P9-EDS-015

Freedom in Faith

A Commentary on Paul's Epistle to the Galatians

by

H. D. McDONALD
Ph.D.(Lond.), D.D.(Lond.)

FLEMING H. REVELL COMPANY
OLD TAPPAN, NEW JERSEY

The Bible quotations in this publication are from the Revised Standard
Version of the Bible, Copyrighted 1946 and 1952.

This book was originally published in Great Britain by Pickering &
Inglis Ltd. of Glasgow.

Library of Congress Cataloging in Publication Data

McDonald, Hugh Dermot.
    Freedom in faith.

        1. Bible. N. T. Galatians—Commentaries.
I. Title.
BS2685.3.M32   1974   227'.4'066   73-23076
ISBN 0-8007-0656-0

In Everything Giving Thanks

Always among the 'everything' are some special things and some persons in particular that call forth thanksgiving.

Special, therefore, must be our thanks to Pickering & Inglis for the trouble and care taken with the manuscript as presented to them, and for its final production.

In particular, therefore, we must thank our son, Neil Martin McDonald, B.D., for finding time amid his heavy schedule of work for his advanced degree in Theology in the University of Birmingham, to read the 'Proofs'.

And with him we must couple Phyllis also who together, 'Help one another to carry these heavy loads'

(Galatians 6.2 NEB).

Contents

CONTENTS

Introduction

It is usual for expositions of the Epistle to the Galatians to be prefaced by a lengthy chapter of introduction dealing with questions concerning its date and destination. But these will not be undertaken here. We will, however, declare ourselves peremptorily on these matters. It is our view that the Galatian letter was among Paul's earliest writings. It may, indeed, have been the very first to come from his pen; in which case it can be placed before the Council of Jerusalem of 49 A.D. of which an account is given in Acts 15. It certainly came before Romans to which it is related as the rough model to the completed statue. It is our conviction, too, that the advocates of the so-called Southern Galatian theory are correct in regarding the churches to which Paul wrote as located in Antioch, Lystra, Iconium and Derbe.

There need be no doubt about the genuine Paulinity of the epistle. It betrays itself throughout to be a message poured forth 'red-hot' from the burning heart of the apostle himself in the form in which it has come down to us.

Something more precise must, however, be said about the occasion of the letter. It is clear from internal evidence that before he wrote to the Galatians, Paul had paid them two visits. On his first coming he was welcomed with enthusiasm (cf. 4. 14f.), and many Gentiles believed. A second visit followed (cf. 4. 13). It was after this second visit that the so-called Judaizers made their appearance among them and sought to persuade the Galatian believers that they had to become subject to the Mosaic law and undergo circumcision if they were really to be saved. These views were reinforced by a challenge to Paul's apostolic authority.

Thus the letter deals with two vital issues. First, the personal one concerning the validity of Paul's apostleship. Paul replies to this challenge with all his apostolic audacity. 'God chose me' (1. 1) and 'God told me' (1. 12) he asserts; and proves his point with compelling reasoning. The other issue, the religious one, concerns the terms on which sinful men are accepted of God. The apostle and his Judaistic opponents alike believed in Christ. But these latter thought that faith in Christ was not enough. They sought to make the gospel a variation of Judaism by contending that observance of the law was a necessary complement to faith in Jesus as the Messiah. The question therefore at issue was a vital one; whether or not for man's salvation faith in Christ needed to be supplemented by circumcision and the keeping of the law. The Judaizers answered, 'Yes'. But Paul returned an emphatic, 'No'. For him, as his own experience of grace disclosed and the revelation which God gave to him confirmed, Christ is the whole of Christianity objectively as is faith the whole of it subjectively.

Had the Judaizers prevailed then Christianity might have survived as a mere Jewish sect, but the gospel would have been lost to the world and man would have remained in spiritual bondage. Galatians was written to bring out into clear light the gospel of grace as God's absolute word to man. It is for this reason that it has been well designated, 'the Magna Charta of spiritual emancipation'. It is the charter of freedom, not only from all forms of legalism, but from every yoke, whether it is ecclesiasticism, traditionalism, rationalism, moralism, asceticism, sacerdotalism, or ritualism, imposed on the religious life as an external condition of salvation.

The fact that this exposition is not addressed to New Testament scholars is so very obvious that it hardly needs mentioning. They have already a sufficient number of learned volumes on this epistle to hand with which to busy themselves. The present commentary is intended for the average Christian, and for the student beginning to come to grips with the New Testament. It is specifically for those who want to work themselves into the heart of this apostolic letter and to ground themselves more firmly in the apostolic gospel. For this reason the Revised Standard Version has been used, as this translation seems to help the modern reader to understand more easily the scriptures of truth, but we will at times find ourselves spilling over in our comment upon the wording of the Authorised Version text.

An Introductory Section — Explanatory

In which Paul Declares his Position

1. 1-9

There is a good deal to be read out of the abrupt way that Paul
begins his letter to the Galatian churches. He took up his pen
under the pressure of a resistless passion stemming out of his
concern for the state of the Galatian believers, and for the
status of the gospel which he had proclaimed to them. What,
therefore, he found necessary to write combined both frost and
fire; for, from the salutation, itself singularly cold towards those
he is addressing, he goes on to express his deep desire for his
'little children' with whom he is in travail once again until
Christ be formed in them (cf. 4. 19). Herein is the mark of a
truly apostolic man; a man who can unite thunder with tenderness. Being such a man, Paul does not hesitate either to present
himself with all his apostolic dignity as God's sent-man, or to
defend his preaching with all his apostolic devotion as God's
sure word. The circumstances require that he wield both sword
and trowel; for he must cut down and build up.

Abrupt, then, is his introductory greeting; for there are no
commendations to be chronicled here. There is no sympathetic
reference to matters of personal interest or individual concern.
There is no note of thanksgiving for the stage reached by these
Galatian churches. The truth is, rather, that they have not
moved up, but stepped down. What thanksgiving could there
be for that? Even the Corinthian believers, indecently tumultuous as they were in their riotous nursery, had some cause for
praise. But the Galatians, removing themselves from apostolic
authority and the faith of the gospel, gave Paul no occasion for

boasting in God. Maybe their church order was correct, and their church membership more exemplary than that of Corinth, but they had allowed themselves to be beguiled into repudiating the authority of God's appointed apostle, and the adequacy of Christ's saving gospel: and these were even more serious matters. This was indeed a spreading disease, which, if not attended to, would speedily kill the church's faith, fellowship and mission. How could Paul commend such a situation as that? How could he condone it? He could do neither. He must, rather, write to those Galatians and do so with all the solemn dignity of his apostolic office. The occasion demanded that he get straight to his purpose with all the overwhelming assurance that he writes as God's man on God's matters.

1

APOSTLE AND GOSPEL

(i) Paul's Commission 1. 1–5

v. 1 Paul, an apostle

The designation, apostle, comes here with a special significance.
It is in his calling as an apostle that Paul writes; here he has his
authority and his right. His apostolic commission had been
questioned among the Galatians and must be upheld against
those who sought to malign and undermine it. At the very
opening of his letter, Paul, therefore, sets down, after his name,
the term which is charged with God's authority and adequacy.
For an apostle was God's specially commissioned man committed
to the task of laying the foundation of Christ's church, and of
building up the church in the faith of the gospel (cf. 1 Cor. 3. 6;
12. 28; Eph. 2. 20; 4. 11; etc.). So Paul addresses himself to the
Galatians as an *apostolos*, to remind them from the first that he
is a man with a divine authority. Because of the occasion, the
emphasis must fall on this word. It was not Paul's habit to
magnify his office; he says elsewhere (1 Cor. 15. 9) that he is
the very least of the apostles, and not worthy to be called one.
He even refers to himself by a term of abhorrence which his
Jewish critics had coined for him, an 'abortion' — a shapeless
form ripped from the womb of Judaism. But it was to such that
the risen Christ 'appeared also' (1. Cor. 15. 8), and that appearance, Paul stresses to the Galatians, is the very source and stay
of his apostleship. He indeed magnifies his office here; but only
for the sake of his God and his gospel.

— not from men nor through man,

A true apostle carries no mere human appointment. So Paul declares at the beginning of his epistle that his apostleship is not from men, nor yet through man (singular). It had not its origin in any human source, nor its authentication in any human agency. Thus was Paul's no second-hand or second-rate apostolate. The false teachers sought to discount Paul's standing as a true apostle of Christ. Right away, Paul asserts that he is: and he makes clear later that he is, in the fullest and most authentic sense, for holding his commission directly from the exalted Lord, it did not come to him from man in general (cf. 1. 11), or from the apostles in Jerusalem in particular (cf. 1. 16, 17). His apostleship is his by a divine right; a gift of grace.

but through Jesus Christ and God the Father,

Here Paul emphasizes that Jesus Christ and God the Father are the direct source and the immediate channel of his apostleship. This fact puts him in a position of equality with those who were commissioned to be apostles before him. Yet, by directing attention to Jesus Christ and God the Father, Paul turns his readers' thoughts immediately away from himself to the divine origin of all such choosings. In this way he places Jesus Christ on a more than human plane. For the words can be read in the light of (i) a contrast. Paul's apostleship is not through *man*, but through *Jesus Christ*. That puts Jesus Christ outside the sphere of mere humanness. Paul's words can also be read in the light of (ii) an association: 'but through Jesus Christ and God the Father'. This name is linked with that of God the Father without any sense of incongruity or strain. For Paul, Jesus Christ quite clearly belongs to the divine side of reality.

who raised him from the dead —

Paul adds this declaration, not just because the thought of God the Father, in conjunction with Jesus Christ, was always associated in his mind with His resurrection from the dead by the Father's loving act, nor because for him the first experience of Christ had been an encounter with the resurrected Jesus. There was a special reason why, at this point, he should refer to the resurrection; for although he may not have seen the Lord in the days of His flesh, as had the other apostles, nevertheless, it was from the risen Christ he had been commissioned to be an apostle. And doubtless, too, that by so presenting, at the beginning, the resurrected Jesus Christ, the way was already prepared for the main theme of the letter; justification in Christ, not by the law (cf. Rom. 4. 25). The declaration regarding the resurrection is made with deliberate intent; for, 'Paul speaking out of the abundance of his heart desires to set at the very beginning "the unsearchable riches of Christ", and to proclaim the righteousness of God which is called the resurrection of the dead' (Luther). He has a twofold purpose in adding these words. His apostolic authority was being impugned, and the fundamental message of the gospel was being perverted. Paul declares that it is the resurrected Christ who assures his apostolic commission, and who guarantees his gospel of man's full acceptance before God by faith. Let the Galatians think of that; — think of the risen Christ, raised by God the Father, of whom Paul is an apostle. Behind his mission and his message stands the reigning Lord.

When did Paul receive his apostleship from Christ? It was certainly in that light-blinding experience on the Damascus road, when the glory of the risen Christ flashed around him. It was then, with his physical eyes rendered sightless, he saw the Lord no longer 'after the flesh'. In 1 Cor. 9. 1 to have 'seen the Lord' is taken as the token of his apostleship.

v. 2 and all the brethren who are with me, To the churches of Galatia:

Who are these brethren Paul can couple with himself in what he has to say to the churches of Galatia? His fellow-workers in the gospel travelling with him (cf. Ac. 19. 29—20. 14); this would seem the most probable answer. But it is difficult to reconcile with the hypothesis of an early date. Besides, the term used by Paul has a deeper significance than the usual one for 'with'; the latter has the idea of bodily presence, whereas the one used here has the notion of a sympathetic bond. Thus would Paul associate with himself those who share his position on his apostleship and his gospel. Accepting the so-called Southern Galatian theory, the churches addressed were located in Derbe, Lystra, Iconium, and Pisidian Antioch.

v. 3   Grace to you and peace from God the Father and our Lord Jesus Christ,

Grace here, as always, is not just for Paul the first word of a conventional salutation, but the very heart of his gospel. At every mention of it, the apostle is laying bare the essence of the good news as he had proclaimed it. It was by God's unmerited favour that he was set out and sent forth as God's appointed man to announce the redeeming message of full discharge to all who have faith. The term 'grace' is Paul's special word; the very summary of his own experience of having being sought by God and brought to God by God's own act of absolute mercy. With grace, Paul associates 'peace', to make that familiar salutation experimental. For it is by grace that peace becomes a reality of life. Peace with God, with ourselves, and with others, is the gift of God's grace.

Paul now changes the order of reference. In verse 1 it is 'through Jesus Christ and God the Father'; here it is, 'from God the Father and our Lord Jesus Christ'. Can there be any significance in the reversal? It may be that he wants to recall to the Galatians, and to have all believers never to forget, that God's grace, which brings man into a state of peaceful relation with Himself, has its fount in God the Father, and comes to us from the Lord Jesus Christ, as its channel, and from Him alone. The 'our' in Paul's statement carries with it a sense of immediacy and intimacy. It is only as He is 'ours' that grace and peace are realized. Once again Paul brings together into an indissoluble unity God the Father and the Lord Jesus Christ; and by the prefix *Lord*, the name given to God in the Old Testament, he heightens for us his estimation of Him of whom he spoke constantly with bent knees and glowing heart. What Paul can say of God the Father, he can say of the Lord Jesus Christ, naturally and truly.

v. 4   *who gave himself for our sins*

In this pregnant statement Paul proclaims anew to the Galatians
the grounds of God's acceptance of sinful men, which they had
virtually forgotten. In this one phrase is gathered up the
fundamental belief of the apostolic church (cf. Gal. 2. 20; see
Rom. 8. 32; 1 Tim. 2. 6; Tit. 2. 14). The keynote of the epistle
is struck in this summary declaration. *He gave Himself* — these
words should be written in red and gold, for they unite sacrifice
and glory. It was *Himself* He gave; nothing more, nothing less.
And who the 'Himself' is, the previous verses have made clear.
He *gave* Himself — gave Himself as a gift, as a sacrificial
offering 'in respect to', and 'on behalf of' man's sins. And it was
our Lord Jesus Christ (v. 3) for *our* sins; ours becoming His
and He becoming ours. Both occurrences of the 'our' should be
underscored, 'for the effect consisteth in the well applying of
the pronouns' (Luther). Our 'sins' — must not that word be
written down in darkest black? Not because of our goodness,
our worthiness, our righteousness did He give Himself up on
Golgotha's tree; but for our sins. That is the reality on which
faith must take its hold; that is the hold by which faith will
maintain its reality.

to deliver us from the present evil age,

The word 'deliver' states what the offering of Himself has
wrought for man. Salvation is of the nature of a deliverance, of a
rescue. The word is used by Paul in Acts (26. 17) in another
connection, and shows one of those 'undesigned coincidences'
between Paul and Luke. Christ's act procures man's rescue
from the fleeting things of this transitory age. The present
period of human history is evil in contrast with that which is to
come; and from it Christ gave Himself to redeem us. The
emphasis falls upon the word *evil*, and the true reading characterizes it as 'the present world of evil'. And it was the evil of the
age which necessitated the giving up of Himself. Man whose
moral and spiritual state is wrapped in darkness, perverted by
ungodliness and dominated by Satan, can only be emancipated
by the mighty atoning act of our Lord Jesus Christ. So He gave

Himself. The world at its best, the religious world, crucified Jesus, so that the world at its best shows how evil is the present sphere of human existence. Yet from it Christ delivers: religion cannot, neither can law.

according to the will of our God and Father;

What is 'according to the will of God'? Delivered? Yes, surely. Then is it not of works or of merit. Thus are the Judaizers shown to be falsifying the gospel of grace. Or, perhaps, the reference is: He gave Himself for our sins to deliver us from the present evil age 'according to the will of our God and Father'. Yes, that, too, certainly. Our emancipation by His self-offering is no less God's will. And if God's will for man's salvation is disclosed in Christ's atoning act then there, and there only, will it be found. There is nothing the Judaizers can add to that.

v. 5   to whom be the glory for ever and ever. Amen.

This is not merely a theological utterance. This is personal religion; a doxology for deliverance. It is out of the deep well of his own profound spiritual experience that Paul sends forth this spontaneous outburst of faith and praise. Whereas Philo was, as Deissmann contends, a lighthouse, Paul was a volcano. Certainly, whenever Paul mentions the salvation that is in Christ Jesus our Lord he erupts in worshipping gratitude. He always writes as a redeemed man; as one whose theology is a theophany. To his doxology he adds a fervent, Amen. Amen in the Hebrew conveyed the idea of firmness, and thus of 'truth'. It then came to be used to express agreement with a prayer or praise offered by another. Here it is employed as an emphatic affirmation; a solemn declaration of all that he has said about God the Father and our Lord Jesus Christ.

(ii)   Paul's Constraint 1. 6–9

Other epistles are followed at this point by a thanksgiving for the progress made by the readers, or such matters as occasion commendation. But it is not so here. Instead of Paul being able to express delight at the consistency of the Galatians, he can only express dismay at their compromise.

v. 6   I am astonished that you are so quickly deserting him

No note of thanksgiving follows the salutation; what comes is rather a passionate outburst of astonishment at the 'shifting' and 'deserting' attitude of the Galatians. He had hoped 'for better things'. But so quickly had the rot set in when the test came. No wonder Paul is 'amazed' (Phillips). Not having taken firm root in the grace of Christ, they 'hastily' began to wilt and wither. The word used by Paul does not, in this context, specify duration (cf. 2 Thess. 2. 2; 1 Tim. 5. 22); he is not indicating anything about the length of time which had elapsed between their acceptance of the gospel and their movement away from Him who called them in grace. The thought is, rather, that they took the very first opportunity, and, it seems, without any real stand against the false teachers, to sidestep from the way of faith. So under this stress they are soon found floundering, drifting, deserting. Yet, by the use of the continuous tense, it is made clear that they had not got to the point of no return. The process had indeed begun, but the climax was not yet reached. It might still be arrested. They may even now return to Him.

who called you in the grace of Christ

Understood here by the 'who' is God the Father. The call is His to make (cf. v. 15; Rom. 8. 30; 9. 24, 25; 1 Cor. 1. 9, 15, 17 etc.). The source of man's salvation is the divine call issued from the very heart of God the Father. And the instrument of that salvation is the grace *of Christ*. The use of the genitive of location (cf. 'righteousness of God' Rom. 1. 17; etc.) directs man to Christ alone. It is in the grace of Christ that the actuality and the assurance of salvation are found. Some prefer to render the phrase, 'by grace', and others, 'unto grace'. But it matters not which, for they are both true: it is all of grace, from first to last; we are called in grace, by grace, unto grace. To desert Him who called them by such grace would indeed mean to be removed from the apostolic gospel. To 'about-face' in the light of such grace would be fatal. To be 'called in grace' must bring to his readers' recollection the amazing wonder of the gospel.

It is a gracious call because it is a call in grace. But it is, however, a call; it is not just a plea for a pitying look, but a divine word carrying obligation on the part of the one who hears. There is a seriousness about the call of God; for there is none more urgent than He.

and turning to a different gospel —

Such would be a 'gospel' without grace; a gospel of which God is not its absolute source and Christ its absolute author. This is the new-fangled teaching which is undermining the faith of the Galatians. This, says Paul with evident sarcasm, is a new sort of 'gospel'; stuff of another brand. What the innovators have to say is so different from the gospel of grace which Paul proclaimed, that their so-called 'gospel' is no good news at all. No false teaching comes, after all, by parading itself as error. The Galatians supposed that their new evangelists came to them in the interests of the gospel; but that 'gospel' of theirs was not Paul's gospel. It was in every way — in its origin, outlook, result — a different message.

v. 7   not that there is another gospel,

Emphatically Paul declares that this different gospel is not another gospel. The syntax of the passage is much discussed, but the sense is clear enough. There is no other gospel than that which the apostle had proclaimed in Galatia at the first. The false teachers say that theirs is *the gospel*, and Paul ironically allows their claim, to refute it. Though I have called it 'a gospel', it is not really so. There is one gospel and no other. The Galatians were attaching themselves to this 'different' gospel which was so radically at odds with the gospel of Christ that it does not merit the name of gospel, and therefore may not be thought of as 'another gospel' at all. The distinction between 'different' and 'another' is that the first indicates a resemblance which it negates; and the second an identity which it negates. The 'gospel' of the false teachers, whether presented in resemblance with Paul's gospel or in identity with Paul's gospel is not his gospel but another. In no sense is it Paul's gospel; and in no sense therefore is it the gospel of Christ.

but there are some who trouble you

The emphasis here is on the persons causing such perversion rather than on the nature of their action. The apostle does not specify who they are; there is no need. Their coming is but recent and their presence among the Galatians is welcomed. But as the letter unfolds the true gospel of Christ they will be further identified. Their intention is to disturb the loyalty of the Galatians to the apostle. To Paul, false teachers were regarded as church troublers.

and want to pervert the gospel of Christ.

Now is disclosed the nature of their evil. They would shake the allegiance of the Galatians and turn the gospel into its very opposite. For by their legalistic demands they were fastening upon men once again the yoke of external conditions for salvation. Such was surely the very antithesis of God's free and full redemption in Christ, which was Paul's gospel; rather, it is the veritable 'gospel of Christ'. This does not mean the gospel proclaimed by Christ, but the gospel of which He is the very centre and essence. In Romans 1. 1 it is the 'gospel of God', and in Romans 1. 9 it is the 'gospel of his Son'.

v. 8   But even if we, or an angel from heaven, should preach to you a gospel contrary to that which we preached to you, let him be accursed.

The Greek of this verse implies a case supposed which has never occurred. The situation is so hypothetical as to be outside the bounds of possibility. The use of the hypothetical — the 'if' construction — is characteristic of this epistle (cf. 1. 9, 10; 2. 14, 17, 18; 3. 4, 18, 21, 29; 4. 7; 5. 2, 11, 15, 18, 25; 6. 1, 3, 9). Here we have a postulate for the preacher. If it were possible that he, Paul, and those who share his gospel were to proclaim any other message; if it were credible that an angel from heaven, a being of such celestial nature, should bring any other word than that which the Galatians had heard at the first, such would be accursed. For the gospel of Christ cannot be changed; and anyone seeking to do so merits the judgement of God. Paul is insisting on the perfection of the gospel. There is none other adequate; and no other authentic. To add to it would be to render it void; thus to preach anything besides that which was preached would be folly, fruitless and fatal. Paul puts himself then into the 'we' of the verse. The gospel that he and others proclaim is not his gospel, but Christ's, which none, even an apostolic man on earth or a ministering spirit from heaven, can alter. It is that unchanging gospel the Galatians had heard, and to remove from it, or to add to it, is to be accursed of God.

v. 9   As we have said before, so now I say again, If any one is preaching to you a gospel contrary to that which you received, let him be accursed.

From the imaginative heights Paul descends to the tragic situation. From the impossible 'should preach' of the angels, his thoughts turn to the actual 'is preached' of the new teachers. It was really being done. It is therefore in the present situation that the words of this verse operated. This is not, consequently, a mere repetition of the previous one. Paul is recalling warnings previously given (cf. 2 Cor. 7. 3), the occasion, perhaps, being his second visit of Acts 14. 21f. They have, alas, drifted from where they were with him; he is anchored where he was before. But anyone preaching a contrary gospel should hear the thunder roll; for if, impossible thought, another gospel should be proclaimed by any other than that which the Galatians had heard from Paul the apostle, it would evoke divine condemnation. And because this is so, what hope of escape can there be for those who are perverting Christ's gospel?

A Personal Section — Apologetic

In which Paul Vindicates his Apostleship

1. 10—2. 15

In this section Paul stresses the divine source of his apostleship
in the gospel. The events of his life show how the faith which
he now preaches could not permit any other explanation than
that God Himself had wrought the change in him. He had been
at one time a stern opponent of the gospel. By upbringing and
in outlook he was a natural enemy of the church. But then,
unbidden and unsought, on the highway to Damascus the light
shone about him; and he found himself Christ's captive.
Touched by the risen Lord in the experience of grace, and
taught by Him in the message of grace, Paul became Christ's
devoted apostle, dedicated to the preaching of His gospel. It was
in the absolute assurance of His divine appointment that Paul
preached the gospel in Galatia. That apostolic gospel the people
of Galatia had openly received and it had wrought a good work
in them. The Judaizers would deny him his standing as God's
apostle that they might have their own teaching accepted. Paul
vindicates his apostleship to have the divine trustworthiness of
his gospel assured.

2

THE GOSPEL WAS REVEALED TO HIM

I. 10–12

v. 10   Am I now seeking the favour of men, or of God? Or am I trying to please men? If I were still pleasing men, I should not be a servant of Christ.

Some commentators would put this verse into close conjunction with what Paul has just said. He has spoken about being accursed for not preaching the gospel. In the light of this fact, and in the light of the sufferings the Galatians knew him to have endured, can they now regard him as a man-pleaser? His strong desire not to be accursed of God shows rather that he is supremely Christ's 'slave'. The words can then be read as a sort of parenthetical expostulation. His opponents apparently accused him of appealing to human interests; of being, like a sophist, bent on winning man's approval. He would satisfy man. Paul indignantly repudiates the charge. In the context of what he has declared in verses 8 and 9; and in relation to all that has befallen him in preaching the gospel the insinuation cannot stand. To be a bondslave of Christ and 'yet' to please man would be incompatible; to think it could be done would be a delusion. The 'still' does not imply that Paul was ever guilty of such conduct, that is, of being a time-server and a man-pleaser, except, perhaps, in his unconverted days. Now and forever he is a preacher of the gospel just because he is a slave of Christ.

The Judaizers may have been saying that by his attitude to the law Paul was loosening its demands. That would commend him to men. Paul retorts that far from his message playing up to people to win their approval, his steadfast adherence to the gospel would prove otherwise. He did not, at the first, tell the Galatians just what they wanted to hear; and he is not doing so now. He spoke out of obedience to God then; and he does so from the same motive in the present situation. In the eyes of man, service for Christ's sake is not likely to call forth peals of adulation.

v. 11   For I would have you know, brethren, that the gospel which was preached by me is not man's gospel.

These words come heavily accentuated (cf. 1 Cor. 12. 3; 15. 1; 2 Cor. 8. 1). The gospel proclaimed by Paul 'is no human affair' (Moffatt). It is not the result of human evolution or the fruit of human musing. It came to him with convincing certainty when the truth broke in upon him on the highway to Damascus (cf. Ac. 9). Paul's gospel is not of man, but for man. It is not after the fashion of man (cf. 1 Cor. 9. 8), or according to mere human principles (cf. 1 Cor. 3. 3). In verse 1 Paul has declared that his apostleship was not devised by any human agency; here he asserts that neither was his gospel. The copula 'is' can be stressed; man's gospel would be transient and changing. But the gospel of the grace of Christ has the quality of permanence and immutability. It always 'is' — contemporary, relevant, adequate.

v. 12   For I did not receive it from man,

Paul continues by amplifying the declaration of the previous verse. For neither did it come to me from man. By his use of the emphatic 'I', Paul seems to be contrasting his experience with those to whom he preached. He was the human instrument or agency in their case; but in his case there was no such (cf. v. 11). Some commentators think that Paul is suggesting that he himself — I myself — no less than Cephas, James and the other apostles, came with no ready-made gospel. This idea, though grammatically possible, is less certain that the interpretation just given.

nor was I taught it,

Paul goes further; not only does he deny that man was the source of his gospel, but that, in his case, he was not even instructed as to the method of its reception. At the time that he became a man-in-Christ, he was made aware that he was chosen of God to carry His name to the Gentiles (Ac. 9. 15).

but it came through a revelation of Jesus Christ.

The 'but' marks a strong contrast. The gospel was not received by him from any human source and it was not taught to him by any human agent: it came by a revelation; not by 'flesh and blood', but by the direct action of the exalted Lord. This is Paul's 'apocalypse' — Christ's own unveiling of Himself to Saul of Tarsus in which he became His redeemed and commissioned man. The genitive has been taken here to indicate the subjective or the objective side of this divine-human encounter. Some think the stress is on Christ as the one who reveals; others prefer to see Him as the One revealed. But why not both? That would certainly suit the purpose and context of the passage. It was Christ who revealed Himself to the apostle; thus it was not 'of man'. He might have received it from God and been instructed therein by man. But Paul denies just that. He received it and was taught it by direct revelation. Both for illumination and instruction Paul was dependent on Christ's own revelation. The enlightenment and the explanation were alike 'of Jesus Christ'.

3

THE GOSPEL WAS EXPERIENCED BY HIM

1. 13–24

That the gospel was in very truth to Paul no human affair communicated by human agency he now sets out to prove by the facts of his own experience. The point of his argument is this: his previous education could not have disposed him favourably toward it, for he was brought up in principles directly opposed to Christ and His gospel (vv. 13, 14). Even after his conversion he remained aloof from the apostles of the Circumcision so he could not have learned of it from them (vv. 15–17). And when at length he did visit Jerusalem, his stay was brief, and his contact with the leaders of the church not specially intimate. He left, still unknown, even by sight, to the majority of the believers (vv. 18–24).

In developing this proof from the details of his personal history, Paul first gives an account of his life

(i) Before his conversion

v. 13   For you have heard of my former life in Judaism,

Of his past career, they had doubtless heard from Paul's own lips. It was part of his testimony, and an element in his teaching (cf. Ac. 22. 2–21; 26. 4–23; 1 Cor. 15. 8–10; Phil. 3. 5–6; 1 Tim. 1. 13). Not only might the Galatians have heard Paul tell of the wondrous change brought about by the revelation of Christ Jesus which had shown up his earlier life for the worthless

26

pursuit it was; but from others, too, they would have heard the story by way of illustration of the transforming power of Christ's gospel. It was in this second way that the churches of Judea which, at the time, had never seen Paul face to face, glorified God because of him (cf. vv. 22–24). It was out of a desire to observe to the full the rituals of Judaism that Paul recalls his past terrifying zeal.

how I persecuted the church of God violently and tried to destroy it;

And how he had persecuted the church of God! (cf. Ac. 8. 1f.; 9. 1f.; 13f.; 24. 4f.). Paul is trying to convey something of the intensity of his work by referring to the violent nature of his persecution. Paul did nothing by half either as a sinner or a saint. There was fury in his action; he put more than ordinary zeal into his terrible work. He 'harried', 'laid waste', 'devastated' God's church. This was certainly a sad recollection for Paul (cf. 1 Cor. 15. 9); the remembrance of it haunted and humbled him. He persecuted the church; the church of God. Paul puts that in by way of contrast and comfort. He, as Saul of Tarsus, daring to set himself against God: the sheer audacity of it! What a contrast is here; '*I* persecuted', 'the church of *God*'. Yet there is comfort in it. For it *is* God's church. It will, then, be all right in His hands. Let the Judaizers recall that it was from the perspective of his Judaism he had persecuted the church of God; that was where he once stood. Now he, Paul, by divine revelation, is Christ's apostle in the church of God: that puts him in the right at the bar of heaven above, and before the church below. The designation the 'church of God' brings out the idea of it being a continuation of Israel as the chosen people of God. And since, as the Galatians themselves were witness to the fact, the church of God was not confined to historic Israel, the one decisive criterion of belonging is faith, and that alone.

v. 14 and I advanced in Judaism beyond many of my own age among my people,

Paul advanced in the legalism of Judaism; but the Galatians had failed to do so in the liberty of Christ. And in his Judaism he was 'becoming a proficient' in all the affairs of Jewish rituals and requirements, outshining those of his own age. The 'young man' Saul (cf. Ac. 7. 58) outstripped all his youthful fellow-enthusiasts in their zeal for the traditions of the elders. Paul was evidently a young man when he was apprehended by the risen Lord: and when, at length, he comes to refer to himself as 'Paul the aged' (Philem. v. 9), he can affirm that he has kept on to the end of the road, with his faith unshaken and his gospel uncompromised (cf. 2 Tim. 4. 6). Paul was quite a young man when he wrote this letter. Here is something which some modern churches should note well. They seek pastors and teachers just beyond the age of youth; they forget that it is not age that matures life, but faith and grace; commitment and devotion; obedience and openness (cf. 1 Tim. 4. 12). The Middle Ages were not the brightest and best of our human history! And middle age is often the time in individual experience when the warm abandonment of youth gives way to cold cynicism. But that was never the case with Paul. Well might he wonder what would be the verdict on the Galatians at the end of their days. They had begun so finely, but had tapered off. It was the apostle's purpose in his letter to recall them to their first allegiance so that when the twilight days came, they, like himself, might magnify the grace of Christ, which could submerge even this dark period of their experience in its forgiving glory (cf. Joel 2. 25).

so extremely zealous was I for the traditions of my fathers.

Paul the Pharisee was indeed a 'Zealot', but not of the political Zealot party. The word followed by the genitive is meant to indicate particularly the direction of Paul's zeal; it was for 'the traditions of his house' (Moffatt) (cf. 'zealous towards God', Ac. 23. 3). Such fervent attachment and devoted activity did Paul show for the inherited ways, that he left others far behind. He adhered without faltering to the traditions of the 'most strictest sect' of the Pharisees (cf. Ac. 23. 5, 6). In the Gospels, the term used for 'traditions' usually carries with it some tinge of disparagement, and seems to refer more particularly to the 'mishna' or traditional interpretations and additions given by the rabbis, rather than to the sacred text itself (cf.

Mt. 15. 3, 6; Mk. 7. 3–13, etc., see Col. 2. 8; but note Ac. 6. 14; 28. 17). Paul refers to the divine prescriptions which were committed to his people by the more venerable term, the Law.

What Paul intends here, is to emphasize the purity and ardour of his pre-conversion religious life, to show that his severance from it to embrace the faith of Christ was of necessity not of human origin and development. In this way, he makes the point that if Paul, the Jew, made a radical break with Judaism, then the Gentiles should realise that to allow themselves to be induced into supposing that the gospel needed any Judaistic additions was sheer folly. His pre-conversion experience demonstrates that adherence to the traditions of his fathers was not the way of grace and faith.

(ii) In his conversion

v. 15 But when he who had set me apart before I was born, and had called me through his grace,

Paul felt himself to be the object of God's special electing purpose. It was a conviction which he held with adoring wonder. He was in the ordaining heart of God before he came under the ordering hand of Christ (cf. Is. 49. 5; Jer. 1. 5; Rom. 9. 11). Before he was born, and certainly before he was 'born again', he had been made God's chosen instrument. He was once a Pharisee, a 'Separatist', now he discovers that he was destined 'to be separated' for a higher and nobler purpose. He was called in the grace of the gospel that he might be a proclaimer of the gospel of grace (cf. Rom. 1. 1). And by 'grace' Paul underscores how unmerited was his relationship to God; it was of God's sheer mercy, not of his sure merit; it was God's work not his.

v. 16a was pleased to reveal his Son to me,

God's unveiling of His Son took place 'within him'; in his innermost soul. It is not just, as in the text, 'to' me. It is out of his enlightened soul that Paul can reveal Christ to the Gentiles. The veil which in Judaism had blanketed his heart was taken away; and there the light 'shined' (2 Cor. 4. 6), to give to him the knowledge of the glory of God in the face of Jesus Christ.

It is by this assertion that God had revealed his Son 'in' him, that Paul makes good his case that his apostleship had been given to him by 'a revelation of Jesus Christ' (v. 12). Paul has no need in the present context to allude to the objective aspect of the revelation of Christ made to him in the Damascus road experience. Lightfoot prefers to translate 'through' him, and he contends that the apostle is not referring to a 'revelation made inwardly to himself, but to a revelation made through him to others'. But this is the point he makes in the next verse. Here, he is emphasizing that so decisively divine was the act by which God disclosed Himself to his soul that he had no need of further human illumination. In that one revelatory encounter there had come to Paul the essential message of the gospel: salvation by grace apart from works in and through the self-disclosure of Christ, the living Lord. All was of God's good pleasure; none of his performance. The Son was revealed directly to him indeed; but to be unveiled directly within him and so to be disclosed directly through him.

in order that I might preach him among the Gentiles,

The revelation was made 'in' him, that it might be made manifest 'through' him. This was part of the electing purpose of grace for him. From persecuting he was turned to preaching. The word translated 'preach' suggests more than the mere act of preaching; something of the content is implied. It is to the Gentiles he preaches; and the note of 'good news' is there. It must be 'good news' for them to learn that they are declared righteous by God's own loving act of mercy. Paul is called of God to show forth these glad tidings. The tense is continuous, for the task is not done. It is to be Paul's full-time occupation to the end of his life. And the process which Paul began is still the church's ever-present duty.

(iii) After his conversion

It is Paul's purpose in this passage to make clear that following his conversion he remained independent of all human authority. He recalls first that there were some things he did not do (vv. 16b–17a).

v. 16b   I did not confer with flesh and blood,

Paul did not straightway seek consultation with any human
being. His apostleship began like Peter's; it came not by 'flesh
and blood' (cf. Mt. 16. 17), but from God direct. Thus given,
Paul realized right away that he had no need for further counsel
of any. It might have been a natural thing for him to have
entered into personal intercourse with those in Damascus who
were already 'disciples of the Lord' (Ac. 9. 1). But this he did
not do —

*v. 17a   nor did I go up to Jerusalem to those who were apostles
before me,*

That, too, might have been a natural thing to have done. And
the way the apostle throws in his negative 'neither' (AV) shows
that he was aware such action might have been supposed likely.
It was usual, apparently, to speak of 'going up' to Jerusalem,
situated as it was on a hill (cf. Ps. 127. 4). But instead of 'going
up' Paul 'goes away'. Like his Lord, in the afterglow of His
baptismal experience, Paul is driven into the 'wilderness'; and
if not, in his case, by the devil, certainly by the Dove that there
he may 'learn Christ'.

Paul recognized, of course, that there were apostles before
him; but in point of time, not of authority. The expression
'apostles before me' implies indeed that Paul, while conscious
as he always was of his own unworthiness to be called an apostle,
places himself within the circle, as having a status no less than
theirs. Such were the things he did not do; but these things he
did (17b–21) —

v. 17b   but I went away into Arabia;

The 'straightway' which appears in the middle of verse 16 is
carried through into this section. After his apprehension by
Christ he was constrained to avoid Damascus and Jerusalem
but instead took off for Arabia. This is the only reference to his
visit to the region. A good deal of discussion has taken place as
to where exactly it was located. Some think it was a district
within easy reach of Damascus to which Paul withdrew. Others,

mindful of the allusion in chapter 4. 25 to Mount Sinai in Arabia, believe that Paul journeyed to a remoter area, to the country known as Arabia Petraea. How long he remained in this comparative isolation, pondering, as it seems, is hard to say. The conjecture is that it was a stay of three years (cf. v. 18 and compare the 'many days' of Ac. 9. 23). But whatever was the length of the period it was of such a duration as to show his independence of the other apostles. Thus was his commission not of their authority or authorization. For instead of going up to meet the apostles in Jerusalem, his path took him further from them.

and again I returned to Damascus.

Fresh from Arabia, he returned in the assurance of his commission and his gospel to proclaim the good news in the very place where he had earlier intended destruction. There he reveals what had been revealed to him; and comes to learn for the first time the cost of discipleship, with the responsibility of apostleship (cf. 2 Cor. 11. 32). Going again to Damascus, Paul began his ministry in the gospel apart from human directing or appointment; the love of Christ alone constraining him and the lordship of Christ alone commissioning him.

v. 18   Then after three years I went up to Jerusalem

For such a period after his conversion, Paul had no contact with the other apostles. By specifying the period, Paul is emphasizing the fact that he accepted the responsibilities of an apostle of Christ from no human source. He had kept away from Jerusalem for three years; kept away in bodily presence, but not surely in spirit. Often must his thought have been there; but not in Solomon's Porch where the disciples were wont to gather; nor yet even in the upper room, sacred as it was, where those who were Christ's earlier apostles came together. But to that Judgement Hall, and out beyond the city to the place called Calvary, Paul's thoughts would turn. For there, he had learned, the very One whom he had been persecuting had become for him, and his brethren according to the flesh, and for the Gentile world beyond, an offering for sin. There, made actual for him and for all, was the forgiving, redeeming and saving grace of God; and for the Gentiles, too — yes, certainly for them. That is part of the revelation of Jesus Christ made to him; and it is for him to declare it to them. That, he has been taught of God, is what happened there in Jerusalem to which now after three years he goes

to visit Cephas,

What is implied by the word which Paul used about the purpose of his going up to Jerusalem and contacting Peter? The verb 'to visit' is found only here in the New Testament. Some would see in the word an echo of our term 'history' and contend, consequently, that Paul went and had a 'history lesson' from Peter. In this way, it is suggested, he would get information regarding the historical details of the life of Jesus whom he had encountered as Lord on the Damascus highway. If, however, this is correct then too much must not be read into the word. For it was Paul's purpose in recording the events of his life to show that he did not receive either his apostleship or his gospel from any man, not even from one of the apostles in Jerusalem. Yet there is no need to deny that in conversation with Cephas he did learn something of the details of the life of Jesus; although it is certainly implied that whatever he did hear added nothing to the fulness of the revelation he had received. Others regard Paul's word as declaring that he simply went up to Jerusalem to acquaint himself with Peter. This may be the general drift of what he wants to convey. The translation 'to visit' leaves the issue vague. This indefiniteness would certainly suit the context. Chrysostom tells us that Paul's word was used by travellers who went to visit great and famous cities. Was this Paul's first holiday since his conversion? Where better for him to go after his time alone in Arabia, and the subsequent period in Damascus, in the interests of the gospel, than to Jerusalem? And who better to see there than Peter?

So Paul visits Peter, or, using as he does his Aramaic name, Cephas. There was, perhaps, a touch of humour in Paul referring to him by that name. For Peter, too, was a Jew, but he was never so committed to Judaism as Paul had been. It will not do for the Judaizers to quote Cephas as authenticating their Judaistic ritualisms. Paul slyly reminds Peter of the Aramaic significance of his name and recalls to him that he bore the Greek equivalent, 'Petros' — a rock. Will Peter be true to that name and remain unshaken always? Paul knows only too well that it is not so and he will find it necessary to oppose him openly as a waverer (cf. 2. 11). The visit paid by Paul to contact Peter was short and apparently not very informative.

and remained with him fifteen days.

There is a whole argument in this specifying of the period. Only for a day beyond two weeks did Paul stay with Peter. And what is fifteen days in comparison with three years! What can be learned in so short a time? Not in that fleeting visit could Paul have been instructed. Indeed, he came knowing for himself the gospel as God's ordained apostle. It was not to be instructed that he came, but to inform. If instruction there was, Peter, as the sequel shows, was the one who stood most in need of it.

v. 19   But I saw none of the other apostles except James the Lord's brother.

James is referred to in Acts 15. 13 and 21. 18 (cf. Mk. 6. 3; Gal. 2. 2, 9, 12). He is not, of course, James, son of Zebedee, who had already passed from the scene wearing the martyr's crown (Ac. 12. 1). This is the brother of our Lord according to the flesh, and the author of the Epistle of James. Now he is a brother of Jesus in the deepest spiritual sense; for he had come to see in Him whom he knew as 'brother' in their Nazareth home, the true Elder Brother (cf. 1 Cor. 15. 7). No longer did James consider important his relationship of blood, knowing now his redemption by Blood. Once he had stood without when it was told to Jesus that His mother and brethren were seeking Him. Who, asked Jesus, are my mother and my brethren? It is those who do His Father's will who are His real and nearest relations (cf. Mt. 12. 46f.). It is not certain whether Paul puts James in the category of apostle. James was certainly not one of the Twelve. Some commentators think that there is hesitancy in Paul's own thought regarding the status of James. They would, therefore, render the phrase translated by 'except' in our text, as 'unless it were': Paul is then asserting that he saw no other apostle, 'unless it were James the Lord's brother' — with the implication, 'if so be he is to be reckoned as such'.

v. 20 *(In what I am writing to you, before God, I do not lie!)*

In this parenthesis, Paul utters a strong asseveration, in view, apparently, of the repeated insinuation of the Judaizers that he had spent a long time under Peter's instruction. What I am writing to you, he declares, is the sheer truth; I swear it before God. Paul is arguing for the validity and independency of his apostleship; it is not a time for equivocation. And Paul, anyway, is not given to that. The stark facts will vindicate the truth that he is God's chosen man with God's own message.

v. 21 *Then I went into the regions of Syria and Cilicia.*

Acts fills out the details here. Hounded out of Damascus, the apostle was conducted by the brethren to Caesarea and thence on to Tarsus (Ac. 9. 30). He was later joined in Tarsus by Barnabas and together they went to Antioch where they continued a whole year in fellowship with the church and in teaching the people (Ac. 11. 25f.). The Caesarea mentioned by Luke is evidently Caesarea Stratonis, the seaport of Jerusalem. After his visit to Jerusalem, Paul, having made Tarsus his headquarters, began evangelistic activity in the regions about, in the northern part of Syria and the eastern area of Cilicia. Such details are clearly not relevant here; for Paul's main concern is to stress his relationship with the other apostles and the length of the period during which he had no contact with them whatsoever.

v. 22 *And I was still not known by sight to the churches of Christ in Judea;*

The only ones he had seen by sight in Jerusalem were Peter and James. The churches in Judea had never seen his face. They had heard about his work of faith and labour of love; but he himself 'remained unknown' to them. He was 'not known', but still he was 'well known'; well known because of the change that had come about in him.

v. 23 They only heard it said, "He who once persecuted us is now preaching the faith he once tried to destroy."

So the story of his conversion was common property. And reference was made to it from time to time as an evidence of what the grace of God can do in the most unlikely life. Our persecutor is now our ally — what a transformation that! He persecuted *us*; but Paul would remember the words he had heard from the highest heaven, 'I am Jesus you are persecuting'. He tried to destroy the faith. And 'tried' is a good word for what he attempted; for try is all he could do. He, Saul of Tarsus, could not really destroy Christ's church. He was not the last to try, and to fail. Once he tried to destroy the faith, now he never tires of preaching it. The term faith preceded by the article is an equivalent for 'the gospel'.

v. 24 And they glorified God because of me.

What pleasure it must have given Paul to recall that! In what Paul had become and in what he was accomplishing they had found occasion for praise to God. But there seems to be a contrast implied by the words. That attitude of satisfaction appears to have passed. Instead of satisfaction there is slander. Why has the change come about? It was not that Paul's gospel had altered, nor yet that his early work had only now come to notice. The cause was rather in the new situation which had developed in Galatia; the teaching of the Judaizers who had come among them stood opposed to that faith which had turned Saul the destroyer of the church into Paul the declarer of the good news. Then, they had glorified God because of him; but now? If they had not heeded those who clouded and clogged the faith they would do so still; and not in Judea only but no less here among the churches of Galatia. That very glorifying of God because of what Paul had become is itself an eloquent argument. It meant that they recognized him for what he was in Judea. The words come pointedly to the Galatians: did the occasion for glorifying God no longer exist? As far as Paul is concerned it is not so. His conduct and his preaching had remained constant. The fault lay not in him but in them. If they have ceased to glorify God because of him it is because they are no longer grounded in the gospel he had proclaimed to them.

4

THE GOSPEL WAS CONFIRMED TO HIM

2. 1–15

In these verses Paul reaffirms that the gospel which he, as an authentic apostle of Christ, proclaims is Christ's true gospel. It was neither, he has contended, man-given nor man-taught. This he re-inforces by further reference to his personal history. Fourteen years have elapsed, during which time he has had no contact with the apostles of the circumcision. At the end of which period he did go up to Jerusalem, but it was not in obedience to any human advice or demand: it was in response to a direct revelation. This visit was a private one but his apostleship was recognized by those other apostles as being of co-ordinate authority with theirs. It was evident that he was appointed of God to preach the word to the Gentiles. Thus was his gospel confirmed as being one with that of the leaders of the Jewish church.

(i) Discussions at Jerusalem

v. 1   Then after fourteen years, I went up again to Jerusalem

From what event are the fourteen years to be dated? Either from his conversion or from the brief visit of 1. 18. The latter seems more probable as the immediate point of reference. The fact that a period of such duration had elapsed since last Paul was in contact with the apostles in Jerusalem is the fact that he wants to emphasize. All through that period Paul had continued his labours among the Gentiles with his position and his preaching unquestioned.Paul's phrase intends to indicate that the period has now ended. Both his mission and his commission are under suspicion. He has validated his apostleship by reference to the details of his life; now he authenticates his gospel by pointing out that for fourteen years he has been proclaiming it to Gentiles. This visit, if 'again' is taken to mean 'for the second time', is that of which Acts 11. 29–30 is the more detailed account (the word for 'again' is, however, missing in some MSS., and even if retained can be translated 'anew' (cf. Jn. 3. 3 RSV; note Jn. 18. 27 where it does not indicate the number of times). But in view of the need for accurate statement involved in Paul's argument it seems best to retain the word 'again', and read it as affirming that now for the second time Paul visits Jerusalem.

with Barnabas, taking Titus along with me.

Barnabas was one of the great souls of the early church — a good man, indeed, and full of the Holy Spirit (Ac. 11. 24). He probably came from Cyprus (Ac. 4. 37). For long he had been closely associated with Paul in his travels and tasks (cf. Ac. 12. 22—15. 39). During the early period of their association it is Barnabas who seems to have taken the lead, so Luke puts Barnabas's name first (cf. Ac. 11. 22—14. 20). Later, Paul takes precedence (cf. Ac. 15. 2f.). On two crucial occasions Barnabas 'brought' Paul with him (Ac. 9. 27; 11. 25). On this visit they are together as partners in the gospel. And with them they *take* Titus. On another occasion they *took* John Mark, but with tragic consequences for them all (cf. Ac. 12. 25; 13. 13; 15. 37f.). Strangely Titus is not mentioned in Acts, but figures a good deal in Paul's second letter to the Corinthians (cf. 2 Cor. 2. 13; 7. 6; etc.; cf. 2 Tim. 4. 10; Tit. 1. 4). He was a Gentile and uncircumcised. His presence was regarded by Paul as in itself a demonstration of the validity of his gospel; and he is consequently introduced in view of the important issues raised by the visit of which he was to become a sort of 'test case'.

v. 2   I went up by revelation;

Paul's going to Jerusalem was in response to a divine disclosure.

He did not go to seek a ruling but to obey a revelation. Frequently in Acts Paul receives direct communication from God either in dreams or visions, or through a prophetic message, or by the immediate action of the Holy Spirit (cf. Eph. 3. 3). Not then as a matter of sheer caprice or on a moment of impulse did he go; but in answer to the higher ordering of God.

and I laid before them (but privately before those who were of repute) the gospel which I preach among the Gentiles,

The phrase 'laid before' does not mean that Paul offered his gospel for possible correction. The only other occurence of the term in the New Testament is in Acts 25. 14, where it has the idea of, 'to communicate', 'to give an account of'. What Paul did was to relate the gospel which he was 'in the habit of preaching' (present tense). There had been no change in his message throughout the years; it was still the same word that had been given to him in the revelation of Jesus Christ.

The purpose of the visit of Paul and Barnabas was to meet in private the leaders of the church. The word cannot be made to mean 'especially'; on the sixteen occasions of its use in the New Testament it always means 'apart', away, that is, from the public gaze and glare. In contrast with the general gathering for discussion of Acts 15, this was restricted to 'men of eminence'. Those who were of repute certainly included James, Cephas, and John (cf. v. 9), although some others may have been in attendance. Their description by Paul of persons of repute might seem to imply a slight tinge of disparagement. But if so, it would be only in the sense that he was negating the exclusive claim which the Judaizers were making by way of excluding him. The passage does, however, reveal a certain respect on Paul's part for his fellow-apostles.

lest somehow I should be running or had run in vain.

At first sight this seems to suggest that there was a lingering doubt in Paul's mind concerning his teaching; a concern which could only be removed by the approval of the apostles of the circumcision. But this reading of his statement would run counter to his whole contention. He knew his gospel to be the veritable truth of God. Paul had no doubt at all on that score. But he has cause for apprehension. He was concerned lest the Judaizers by insisting on their Mosaic rituals and rules would 'render useless' his whole work. For, after all, the gospel cannot be a transforming message of grace if it is leavened with legalism. Paul had no wish to see his efforts, past and future, brought to nought; and that tragic result would follow with all the greater ease and certainty were the Jerusalem church to insist that Gentile Christians must accept circumcision as a binding condition of their salvation. Thus Paul had come to Jerusalem, not to expound his gospel but to vindicate the application of it to the Gentiles.

Titus has just been introduced, and the passage which follows has to do with the 'case of Titus'. Verses 3 to 5 are among the most difficult in the whole New Testament to exegete, due to our inability to be sure of the meaning of the section, and because of the uncertainty about the text and grammar. It is, according to Lightfoot, a 'shipwreck of grammar'. It is clear, however, that a demand had been made for Titus's circumcision; a demand which raised the fundamental question of the freedom of the Gentiles under grace (Titus was a Greek). But how did Paul meet the demand? Was Titus circumcised? On the one side are those who think that the passage clearly indicates that he was not. For such, verse 3 appears explicit. They regard the case of Timothy's circumcision which Paul sanctioned (cf. Ac. 16. 3) as not parallel; for Timothy's mother was a Jewess, and for him to be circumcised was no sacrifice of principle. Others, however, take the opposite view and contend that Titus did undergo circumcision. These refer to chapter 5, verses 10 and 11 as evidence that the apostle had altered his stance on the matter in the light of the growing demand to make it necessary for the Gentiles. Titus's circumcision, they argue, had been a temporary expedient. The words of verse 5 'we did not yield subjection for a moment' are then taken to mean 'we did not yield to the principle which they were advocating, namely, that of subjection to legalism; our action was but a concession to the necessity of expediency'. But the more natural, and we believe the correct reading of verse 5 is that Paul refused to have Titus

circumcised under any pretext. Not for a moment did he enter-
tain the idea; not for any reason would he permit it, lest the
truth of the gospel should be compromised, and the contention
of the false brethren, who had slipped in to spy out Gentile
freedom in Christ, be given credence.

*v. 3   But even Titus, who was with me, was not compelled to be
circumcised, though he was a Greek.*

The case of Titus was evidently for Paul a crucial one. Titus
was a living proof that his work was not fruitless; the fact of his
presence was a reminder that the position Paul had maintained
regarding the exemption of Gentiles from Jewish legalism had
been approved. The phrase 'who was with me', or, as the NEB
has it, 'my companion', has here an argumentative force. As
Paul's attendant, Titus would of necessity have moved among
Jewish Christians; and he did so as an uncircumcised Gentile
believer. But 'not even' he was compelled to undergo the
circumcision rite of Judaism. And if not he, then why should
others of Gentile birth? The very fact of Titus's presence was
sufficient evidence that a principle had been already established.
Here, the word 'circumcision' appears for the first time in the
letter almost incidentally. But in such a way, nevertheless, as to
show that it was the main platform on which the legalists fought
for the necessity of Gentiles to conform to Mosaism.

v. 4   But because of false brethren secretly brought in,

The thought here is not easy to follow. But the idea seems to be
this: there was evidently pressure upon Paul to have Titus
circumcised, a pressure which may well have come from those
who were of repute and who were themselves being influenced
by certain others — 'false brethren' as Paul saw them to be.
What harm would there be in Titus being circumcised, thus
dispelling the possibility of dissension? Why not do so as a
matter of expediency? Why not? But Paul knew why not. These
false brethren would not regard it in that light, but would see it
rather as a vindication of their own position. Paul's refusal to
concede, lest the principle of freedom in faith should be
compromised, evidently carried these hesitators with him. And

by so doing, the truth about Paul's opponents stood revealed. They were 'false brethren' indeed; not in fact true brethren in Christ at all (cf. 'false apostles', 2 Cor. 11. 13, and 'false prophets', 2 Pet. 2. 1). They were such because they wanted to be Jews outwardly, but failed to be Christians inwardly. They were bound-men in legalism not free-men in Christ. Such were they

who slipped in to spy out our freedom which we have in Christ Jesus, that they might bring us into bondage —

They came in as 'brethren'; but they came in disguise. They had no warrant to come in; and their design was to war against those who had been set free by Christ that they might bring them again under the yoke of bondage. They slipped in secretly, but they slipped up disastrously. For Paul saw through their sham robes, and unmasked them as 'false' intruders. What faith finds in Christ is freedom, liberty, emancipation. But they would reduce whom they could to slavery, bondage, imprisonment (cf. 4. 25).

v. 5   to them we did not yield submission even for a moment,

To these 'false brethren' Paul refused to give way. To them he would not 'submit', whether they sought to gain their purpose either by demand or taunt. This was an issue over which the apostle could make no compromise — 'not for a moment', as the literal translation should be (cf. Jn. 5. 35; 2 Cor. 7. 7, 8; Philem. 15). Yet Paul, when the occasion does not involve him in a sacrifice of principle, is not so scrupulous. Not for an hour, but for any length of time he becomes as a Jew to the Jews, and as under the law to those under the law, if so be he may win them to Christ (cf. 2 Cor. 9. 20f.). Paul's refusal to submit reveals his own certainty of the divine authority of his apostleship and the divine source of his gospel. He repudiated, therefore, the claims of the false brethren that no damage might be done to the word of truth.

that the truth of the gospel might be preserved for you.

Here is the spiritual reason why Paul could not yield. He would preserve 'the truth of the gospel'. The gospel is more than a subjective impression. It has an objective reference. It comes with a truth-content, with a propositional element. It has, therefore, its fundamental doctrinal statements, which to deny, is to place oneself among the 'false brethren' (cf. Col. 1. 5). Grace and truth came by Jesus Christ (Jn. 1. 14); it is by maintaining the truth of the gospel that the true gospel is preserved. It was Paul's one desire to keep the message of Christ intact so that the Gentiles might be free in faith. The 'you' will, of course, include the Galatians; but no less surely all the churches of God whether in Galatia or elsewhere, or whether begun by him or not. The phrase translated 'be preserved for you' can also be rendered 'may abide with you'. The gospel is only preserved for us as it abides with us. Indeed, the word for 'be preserved' (AV 'continue') is intensive. The gospel is 'maintained' (NEB) if it 'remains through' us; that is if it has its home within by being appropriated in faith.

v. 6   And from those who were reputed to be something (what they were makes no difference to me; God shows no partiality) — those, I say, who were of repute added nothing to me;

Here Paul takes up again from verse 2. He had gone to Jerusalem in response to a revelation from God; and there he laid before 'those who were reputed to be something' the gospel he was in the habit of preaching. They could do nothing but accept it. Those held in esteem were 'looked upon as authorities'. However right was the credit, and Paul is not really contesting that, these 'authorities' had no addition to make to his gospel. They had no fresh knowledge to communicate; and they had no further confirmation to give to his position as Christ's apostle. The RSV rightly places the reference to God's impartiality in brackets. Paul began with a statement concerning the gospel which he had set before those 'who were reputed to be somewhat' in Jerusalem. The very idea of a suggested prestige compels him to break off to make the point that human reputation does not affect any man's standing before God. What these men of rank once were can in no way alter Paul's place or proclamation. Certainly, these 'pillars' of the church had the advantage of being eyewitnesses of Christ's life in the flesh, but even that Paul could not allow to be used to induce him to dilute his message. In order to discredit Paul's position, his detractors may well have held back the fact that these men were in personal attendance upon their Lord during His earthly ministry, and had heard from His own lips their call to be His apostles. But Paul does not recognize the claim that such a privilege gave these esteemed men a monopoly of God or an exclusive place in His purpose. Was it not such a claim on God that these very men had heard repudiated by Christ Himself when He was with them (cf. Mt. 20. 21f.)? The same point can be made by Paul. God does not judge men by outward advantage or rank. There is no partiality with Him. He does not accept any man for his status or his attainment. By putting the word 'face' or 'person' first in his statement, Paul throws the emphasis upon the fact — the person of man God does not accept. No one is commissioned because he is 'reputed to be somewhat'. To have known the historic Jesus is not a passport to an exclusive privilege. Office, even in Christ's church, does not put God in any man's debt. And anyway, whatever prestige was accorded to them these men were unable to detract from Paul's testimony to the fulness of the revelation which had been given to him by the resurrected Jesus.

v. 7   but on the contrary,

But 'contrariwise' (cf. 2 Cor. 2. 7; 1 Pet. 3. 9), instead of adding anything to Paul's gospel they found themselves in total agreement with him. Indeed, the contrast suggests something more — there was a certain compellingness about the facts which Paul unfolded.

when they saw that I had been entrusted with the gospel to the uncircumcised,

'When they came to see', that is; for it may well have been that there had been doubt in some minds regarding Paul's position. And this hesitancy was being exploited by the Judaizers. Now, however, the fact stood out crystal clear; now no lingering uncertainty remained. What Paul had stated in solemn truth carried full conviction. The whole circumstances of Paul's conversion by God's immediate act, the content of the gospel he proclaimed among the Gentiles, the undoubted results his message produced, and the calm and careful spirit in which he stated his case, all combined to secure the fullest agreement that he had been entrusted with the gospel by divine appointment. And by the use of the perfect tense Paul would underscore the permanent nature of that commission. Paul always considered that he had been given the gospel as a 'trust': thus was he a debtor to those to whom he was especially set apart to serve in the gospel, the Gentiles. If it is the gospel of grace he has for the uncircumcised, circumcision is, by implication, ruled out.

just as Peter had been entrusted with the gospel to the circumcised

In each case 'the gospel' is the same; for there is no other gospel but the one gospel of Christ. It was in fact the reality of the 'essential identity' of the good news, whether proclaimed by Paul to the uncircumcised or by Peter to the circumcised, which was seen by those who met for discussion with Paul at Jerusalem. Both men were seen to be divinely commissioned men in their separate spheres. Only in this respect was there any diversity. Each had his own area of operation, and, maybe, too, his own method of presentation, but there was no variation about the basic facts and the blessed fruits of the gospel. Paul, by divine appointment and anointing is set forth as the apostle of the Gentile church, and Peter, in like manner, as the apostolic head of the Jewish church: thus there is no head of the whole church of God except Him who abides as Lord. And there is one gospel, the same for Peter and Paul, in neither case differing absolutely in type and tendency.

v. 8 (for he who worked through Peter for the mission to the circumcised worked through me also for the Gentiles),

In this parenthesis Paul is bringing into outright confirmation what is implied in the previous verse. Paul allows without question Peter's apostleship. But he still insists that he and Peter are on common ground through God's special operation

— 'for he who worked in Peter unto apostleship to the circumcised worked also in me unto apostleship to the uncircumcised'. The apostleship of both is a divine creation, an activity of God (cf. 1 Cor. 12. 6; Phil. 2. 13). It is God, therefore, who is implied in the opening phrase, 'for he who'. This, known as a certain fact in the experience of both apostles, was brought out into clear perception in the discussion. It was something that all could see; God had been working in Peter for the triumph of the gospel among the people of Israel; and so, too, for the same reason had God been working in Paul among the Gentiles (cf. Ac. 15. 12).

v. 9   and when they perceived the grace that was given to me,

In verse 7 we have 'when they saw', here it is 'when they perceived'. There is little difference between the two verbs in the New Testament generally. Yet, perhaps, in this passage a difference of stress was intended. What they *saw* was based on the empirical evidence which Paul adduced — his sight of the risen Lord and the success of the gospel among the Gentiles. Such were outward tokens of his divine commission. They thus *perceived* with a certain compelling conviction that grace had been given to him. Paul's apostleship in the gospel was for them a living demonstration that God has no favourites. It is always the essence of 'grace' that it is something 'given'. By so amplifying 'grace' as 'given', Paul takes delight in emphasizing the undeserved nature of it: and to acknowledge that it is of grace, is to acknowledge that it is 'of God'. It was in this light that they came to perceive it.

James and Cephas and John, who were reputed to be pillars,

James, the head of the church in Jerusalem, Cephas, the apostle to the circumcision, and John, known as the apostle of love; these three — and the greatest of these is — but who can say? Yet all unite in the conviction that Paul's mission and message are 'from above'. Strangely, James comes first in the list, perhaps because of his position in the Jerusalem church, or maybe it was because he took the lead when it was a matter involving practical doctrinal issues. Once again Paul prefers to use the Aramaic, Cephas, instead of 'Peter', for the apostle to the circumcision. Only in two of his seven references does he use the Greek name, Peter (cf. 2. 7, 8). But there was more than mere habit in the preference here. The Judaizers, out of a morbid desire to accentuate their Hebrewism, evidently used the Aramaic form. Paul does likewise, but to show that their Jewish Cephas, apostle to the circumcised though he is, is at one with those who saw that he was entrusted with the gospel and perceived the grace of God that was given to him. With Cephas is associated John. The absence of any detailed reference to John the apostle in the Book of Acts is astonishing (cf. 3. 1; 4. 13; 8. 14). But he is here — as the living presence of love personified. For it is in love that God can enlighten. It would be too fanciful, of course, to see in the trio mentioned here the concrete embodiment of faith, hope and love. Yet it is in love that faith has its source and in hope its strength. It is love, as a willingness to admit and accept the truth about another, which illuminates the eyes to see and instructs the mind to perceive. These three, James, Cephas and John, were reputed to be 'pillars'. The word was common among the Jews as a description of their great teachers. The idea enshrined in the term is best uncovered by its use in 1 Timothy 3. 15. As 'the church of the living God', its proper function is that of 'a pillar and bulwark of the truth'. Upon the church of the living God divine truth is based and built. So in this Galatian passage, this named trio were regarded as the upholders of the truth of the gospel. And it was they who could add nothing to Paul; it was they who saw that his claim was right and who perceived that his gospel was true.

gave to me and Barnabas the right hand of fellowship,

Here was an expressive gesture of mutual recognition and participation. It could be almost translated that they 'gave pledges' to each other, as by the use of the plural Paul directs attention to what is betokened rather than to the outward action. There is here no suggestion of subjection; but rather a demonstration of fellowship. The Judaizers talked about Paul being forced to subject his gospel to the Jerusalem authorities. But by extending to him their right hands in fellowship the very oppo-site was the case. They were clasped in a united faith and a common task. Theirs was not an enforcement from a superior authority but a recognition of appointed spheres.

that we should go to the Gentiles and they to the circumcised;

It was mutually agreed that Paul and Barnabas were to go unto the Gentiles. This was but the recognition of what was already happening. The others would continue their apostolic work among the circumcision. This conclusion to the discussion comes here as a sort of triumphant vindication of Paul's position. Man's freedom in the faith of the gospel, the principle for which the apostle had stood, was affirmed, not only against the con-tinued tumultuous opposition of the Judaizers, but also against the first timid vacillation of the Jerusalem leaders.

v. 10   only they would have us remember the poor, which very thing I was eager to do.

The expressed desire that Paul should remember the poor shows how much the early leaders had come to recognize the social implications of the gospel. The 'only' is, however, suggestive. This was the 'only' stipulation they could make. They could not add one thing to make Paul's apostleship any more authentic or his gospel any more authoritative. This 'only' they could say, 'remember the poor'. Yet this was not a sort of afterthought; it reveals how deeply the church felt about those in need.

In Paul's case, however, there was no 'prompting' needed on this score. This he was zealous to do; this was ever his 'heartfelt desire' (cf. Ac. 11. 29f.; 24. 17; Rom. 15. 25f.; 1 Cor. 15. 1; 2 Cor. 8. 9).

(ii)   Dissension at Antioch

Paul has been, in the previous verses, vindicating his position negatively by showing how he had acted independently of human authority. Now he states his case more positively. As at Jerusalem, so now at Antioch, he asserts that he has the interests of the Galatians very much at heart. What he had won at

Jerusalem he vindicates again at Antioch. Neither directly nor indirectly had Paul's faith and word come to him from a human source or through a human channel. None could, of course, deny that the apostleship and doctrine of the Jewish churches were from God. But how were the two related? Were the apostleship and gospel to the Gentiles fundamentally one with that of the Jewish churches? There would, of course, be outward differences between the general religious attitudes of the Jewish Christians, who still retained in their daily practices and usages Mosaic forms and ceremonies, and the Gentile believers, whose whole outlook was shaped by a different mould. For them the question was, did they, as Gentile believers, need to adopt these Mosaic forms and ceremonies? Paul's own experience of and his service in the gospel made him sure that there was no such need. But was such a declaration of independence ultimately at one with that of the churches of Judea? Was the verdict of heaven equally evident in Paul's case and in Paul's message as it was in Peter's? The leaders of the Jewish churches agreed at Jerusalem that they were. Yet, in spite of this conviction, they went on to put themselves in a position which compromised their verdict. Cephas, with particular reason, and 'even Barnabas', with painful recall, had to be rebuked for this inconsistency; for acting out of accord, and in compromise of what they knew to have been an established principle. But whether in discussion at Jerusalem or in dissension at Antioch, Paul maintains, throughout, his stand for the Christian's freedom in faith.

v. 11   But when Cephas came to Antioch I opposed him to his face, because he stood condemned.

This visit of Peter to Antioch took place evidently after the Jerusalem debate. The actual time is not easy to fix. Peter's connection with the church of Antioch is, however, certain, not only because of this passing allusion to his visit there, but because of the strong tradition preserved in Eusebius and Jerome that the church at Antioch was actually founded by him and that he was its first bishop. The verse comes here like a blow in the face after the warm handshaking episode of v. 7. Yet it is true to Peter's nature to vacillate between standing on the rock and sinking in the waves; sometimes firm and sometimes fickle. Whatever may have been Peter's relationship to the church at Antioch it was the citadel of Gentile Christianity, where believers first received their nickname, 'Christians' (Ac. 11. 26). If Antioch did indeed owe the gospel to Peter — and he seems on this occasion to have come there by some right — then all the more serious was his inconsistency. As he stood 'face to face' with Paul, he found himself condemned in the afterlight of their last encounter.

The issue, however, raised by the next few verses was not quite that which had been central in the Jerusalem discussion. It was not primarily one of the admission of Gentiles into the church, but concerned 'table-fellowship' between believing Jews and Gentiles. It was a practical problem. Peter's withdrawal could only mean division in the church. From the beginning, Peter found it difficult to associate with Gentiles (cf. Acts 11. 2f.). But he had overcome his timidity at least for a season, and at Antioch, where the Gentiles were more numerous, had entered into cordial relationship with the non-Jewish believers. On the coming, however, of certain 'emissaries from James' he shrank back from public association with them. These partisans of James are seemingly not to be identified with the extreme Judaizing group who demanded circumcision for Gentiles. They insisted, indeed, that Jews should act according to Jewish customs in dealing with Gentiles.

v. 12 For before certain men came from James, he ate with the Gentiles; but when they came he drew back and separated himself,

These 'men from James' seem to have come with the approval, certainly, and under commission, possibly, of the leader of the Jerusalem church. They were typical of what we know about the outlook and attitude of James. Before their coming Peter had acted with Christian charity in accordance with the principles of Christian freedom; 'but when they came', things began to change. Under their influence, Peter's cordial companionship with the Gentile believers became more and more strained. The tense of the verbs show that there was a gradual movement away from fellowship on Peter's part to a position of complete separation from those of non-Jewish origin. It could have been that these 'men from James' had never done any other than eat among themselves and when they came down to Antioch they continued the same practice and Peter was impressed. But they do seem to have come with a certain intent; and Paul's stinging rebuke of them suggests that their presence in Antioch was of set purpose in preventing full accord and unimpeded fellowship between Jewish and Gentile believers.

fearing the circumcision party.

There lay the reason for Peter's attitude. Cowardice was Peter's besetting sin. Here once again he shrinks from open declaration of the truth he had already acknowledged. He allowed himself to be tyrannized by a vocal minority. This was the section of Jewish believers — those from the circumcision — who were more concerned with safeguarding their own Jewish social rituals than they were with strengthening the Gentile believers.

v. 13   And with him the rest of the Jews acted insincerely,

The other Jewish Christians at Antioch influenced by Peter's ignoble example took their cue from him, and they, too, refrained from associating with their Gentile brethren. In Paul's eyes it was an act of sheer hypocrisy on Peter's part. It was a piece of play-acting; a cloke under which Peter concealed his true feelings and understanding. But Paul was not awed by Peter's supposed infallibility, he was, rather, appalled by Peter's stupid irresponsibility. Peter's insincerity drew into the same shameful game the rest of the Jewish believers. There was no real conviction about the attitude they adopted; it was a pose prompted by fear rather than a principle adopted from faith.

so that even Barnabas was carried away by their insincerity.

Even Barnabas — it is hard to convey the feelings that must have welled up in Paul's heart as he wrote these words. He had been indebted to Barnabas for so much, and they had been together in faith and fellowship over many long years and through many dark paths. Even Barnabas — *et tu, Barnabas!* — Paul could hardly believe it; he did not really want to believe it. He tried to understand. Barnabas was carried away, swept along as in a flood tide. Yes, that was it; it was a resistless wave, and Barnabas could not keep his feet. Grief, love, hope, sorrow all mingle in that 'even Barnabas'.

v. 14 But when I saw that they were not straightforward about the truth of the gospel,

Paul saw, what they were all blind to, that the truth of the gospel was at stake. For they 'were not going straight according to the gospel'; they were deviating — getting out of step. They had not 'an eye to the truth of the gospel'; neither to its content nor to its extent. The 'truth of the gospel' (cf. v. 5) is the true message which the good news embodies, of man's justification through union with Christ by faith. And by not being 'straightforward about the truth of the gospel' its doctrine was being diluted, and by not 'going straight according to the gospel' its effectiveness was being nullified.

I said to Cephas before them all, 'If you, though a Jew, live like a Gentile and not like a Jew, how can you compel the Gentiles to live like Jews?'

Paul here fulfils his own provision and reproves Cephas 'in the sight of all', that is, 'publicly' (cf. 1 Tim. 5. 20). And he was appealing to a point of fact. Peter was Jewish but he had learned to live with the Gentiles without recourse to Jewish customs and prohibitions. At Antioch he had begun to live in the same freedom of faith and had not erected partition walls between himself and his Gentile brethren. And if he could so live then, why does he act now in blatant contradiction of the principle he has admitted and on which he has acted? How utterly inconsistent of him here at Antioch, first to enter into fullest fellowship with the Gentiles and then, persuaded by those who came from James, to withdraw from them! Peter did not, perhaps, see the real consequence of his strange behaviour. And those who claim him as their pope must see him as a pope in a muddle.

The extreme party, the Judaizers, said the Gentiles must be circumcised to be saved. But that denies the apostolic doctrine of justification in Christ. The party of James said that Gentiles must be separated from fellowship. But that is to deny the unity of believers in Christ. Paul rejected both. Justification is free to the Jew in spite of his customs and to the Gentile in spite of his being without them. And because that is so, Jewish customs are not an integral part of justification, nor is absence of them a hindrance to it. This, Peter had learned and acknowledged; and had demonstrated as a principle of action by not permitting Jewish customs to bother him or to block his fellowship with Gentile believers. Yet he acts 'insincerely', since, knowing that before God custom counts for nothing, he now seeks to compel Gentiles to adopt Jewish ways.

v. 15   We ourselves, who are Jews by birth and not Gentile sinners,
'We' — I, Paul, and you, Peter — are both Jews by birth. That carried with it, as both knew well, its own sense of privilege and status. In contrast with the Gentiles, who can claim no divinely communicated law we, Jews by birth, we, Paul and Peter, have this Jewish heritage and all that goes with it. The Gentiles, in Jewish eyes, were 'sinners', although it should be added that the term referred to ritual rather than to moral delinquency. Yet Paul introduces it here as if to give the designation prominence (cf. v. 17). For it is those who know themselves to be sinners who are in line for justification by faith, whether they be Jew or Gentile sinners. This is in fact Paul's point. I, Paul, and you, Peter, grew up authentic Jews with all that meant by way of privilege and status — but what of it? Nothing at all as regards our standing before God. Both had the truth of the gospel revealed to them, so that Paul can confirm that 'We ourselves, who are Jews . . . know that a man is not justified by works of the law but through faith in Jesus Christ, even we have believed in Christ Jesus, in order to be justified by faith in Christ'. How fundamentally wrong, then, for Peter to act out of accord with that which he knew and had believed!

A Doctrinal Section — Polemical

In which Paul Clarifies his Gospel

2. 16—4. 31

In this, the main part of his letter which begins almost abruptly at this point, Paul expounds the message which had been given to him as God's commissioned apostle. He had been retelling the story of his encounter with Peter at Antioch, but before he is through it appears that Peter is forgotten. He has been lost sight of in Paul's passionate outpourings concerning man's standing before God. Verse 14 of chapter 2 is Paul's answer to Peter's equivocation and vacillation. What follows may be regarded as either the apostle arguing or musing with himself with an indirect reference to the Gentiles or a freely reported account of the continued discussion. In any case, it is not easy to be sure where the break comes. This, however, is clear: throughout the whole section Paul is contending that works and ceremonies are inconsistent with the redemption which is in Christ Jesus. In this Galatian letter he maintains this truth against Judaism: in 2 Timothy the same position is taken up against paganism (cf. 2 Tim. 4. 16, 17).

5

THE WAY OF FAITH

2. 16—3. 5

The main thought in these verses is that justification by faith is
God's declared method of saving men. It is, therefore, neither
within the law's power or purpose to bring man to God. It is
entirely from God's side alone a matter of grace; and on man's
side a fact of faith.

(i) Justification by Faith Declared

v. 16 yet who know that a man is not justified by works of the law

This is something that Peter knew as well as Paul. For the first
time in this epistle the word 'justify' occurs. Yet it is one of the
most significant terms in Paul's theology; and a correct understanding of its meaning is vital for a right understanding of Paul's
gospel. It is essentially a forensic word with the significance of
'to pronounce righteous'. It certainly does not mean 'to make
righteous'. Some scholars would indeed deny that it ever can be
translated in this way. It is apart from works of law that God
accepts a man as approved in His sight as righteous. The verb is
put in the present tense because Paul is enunciating a general
principle. The preposition 'out of' is placed before 'the works of
law' in the original Greek. The declaration that justification is
not by this method is thus strengthened. That righteousness, by
which a man is accepted by God, does not derive from the
fulfilment of any legal enactments. No man gets to be holy,
guiltless and approved in God's sight as a consequence of things

done in obedience to His positive law. By the works of the law Paul means, of course, works wrought to fulfil law with the view of making oneself acceptable to God.

but through faith in Jesus Christ,

Righteousness is not *gained* by works of law — the term *nomos* (law) is anarthrous throughout the section — but it is *got* through faith in Christ Jesus. It is 'through' faith. Faith is not itself the ground of man's justification, but its channel. The preposition has the idea of motion; it is by means of faith in Christ Jesus that a man is taken up into a new relationship with and standing before God. Contrary then to what the Judaizers have to say, Paul declares, 'we teach faith'.

even we have believed in Christ Jesus, in order to be justified by faith in Christ,

By putting the verb 'we believed' in the aorist tense, Paul is pointing to a time when he and Peter 'became believers'. It was then and in this way that acceptance before God was assured. And what holds for them, holds for every man, whether Jew or Gentile. In the preceding clause Paul, as we have seen, has asserted that the only means of justification is 'through' faith in Christ Jesus; he now uses the preposition 'out of' to point to the exclusive source of justification and so eliminates all other possibilities.

and not by works of the law, because by works of the law shall no one be justified

The law is, of course, the Mosaic law taken as an expression of all and any law. The declaration is a strong one; no works of law have effect in making a man approved of God. This is followed by an absolute conclusion 'because by works of law shall no flesh be justified'. These words are a free rendering of salm 143. 2 which is also quoted in Romans 3. 20. In both ssages the 'out of works of law' is a comment of the apostle's, ribing the condition of the person there addressed. It is an axiom of Scriptural theology that by the deeds of law no justified. Thus stand opposed the two ways, the way of faith and the way of law, and there is no contact or compromise possible between them. Inevitably, Luther will have a long comment on this central verse in the Galatian letter in which the apostle states the whole body of saving divinity. In one passage in his lengthy exposition there comes a statement which sums up all he has to say. 'Wherefore Christ apprehended by faith, and dwelling in the heart, is the true Christian righteousness, for the which God accounteth us righteous, and giveth us eternal life'. That is sound Pauline theology; the very heart of the apostolic gospel.

v. 17   But if, in our endeavour to be justified in Christ, we ourselves were found to be sinners, is Christ then an agent of sin? Certainly not!

Paul would seem to be either still opposing Peter in verbal confrontation or arguing with himself about the logical results which follow from the endeavour to be justified in Christ. Those who would be accounted righteous before God may seek it and shall find it, 'in Christ'. This union with Christ is the cause and sphere of our justification. The great theme then of the apostle's message becomes focused in the thought of being 'in Christ'. Yet to endeavour to be justified 'in Christ' apart from the works of law (v. 15) is nothing less than to set the law aside; virtually to violate its prohibitions. And doing that would be, in Jewish eyes, to make oneself a sinner. So be it, you can almost hear Paul say. Thus are we ourselves, I, Paul, and you, Peter, 'found to be sinners'. And to think that Peter had come to treat the believers at Antioch as Gentile sinners, unfit to eat with, because they had not come under the works of the law, when he, himself, seeks justification in Christ by faith, which means the repudiation of the works of the law! Think of that! Yet the plain fact is that it is we, the law-havers, who are the law-breakers. We are the 'sinners', Paul declares, with a touch of sarcasm. But would not that, interjects the possible or actual objector, be to make Christ an agent of sin? Not a bit of it, Paul retorts. God forbid! (cf. 3. 21; 6. 14; Rom. 3. 4, 6 etc.).

This verse has occasioned much discussion among commentators. The question is, What exactly is intended by it?

There are broadly two possible approaches, each of which would seem to give an equally valid understanding of what was in the apostle's mind.

(a) To counter an attack: the Judaizers may well have attacked along this line Paul's great doctrine of justification by faith. Their argument would then be: this preacher to the Gentiles is declaring that all men are accounted acceptable before God apart from law, and that we, who are Jews by nature, must abandon our works of law, our legal way of gaining righteousness, if we would be saved. But to abandon the law is sinful. Does not, then, the assertion, that to believe in Christ for justification it is necessary to repudiate the works of the law, make Christ a minister of sin? To that, Paul answers an emphatic 'Certainly not!'

(b) To deny a conclusion: the point here is, to accept the fact that to abandon law is to be found a sinner, the conclusion that must follow is that Christ is a minister of sin. The thought runs like this: to seek justification in Christ is indeed to reject works of law as the legal grounds of righteousness. The law-keeping Jew would regard himself as 'not a sinner', for the law-keepers are the righteous. The Gentiles are 'the sinners', because they have not and know not any law to keep. But if the Jews, as law-keepers, must abandon law to be justified in Christ, they would become 'sinners', by becoming law-breakers. Would not that be to make Christ the minister of sin? For Paul, the very suggestion that such an idea could be entertained for a moment is repudiated with horror. It is a glaring *non sequitur*.

v. 18   But if I build up again those things which I tore down, then I prove myself a transgressor.

Paul here enters a counter argument. To revert to law, as some desire, and certainly Peter is in mind here, would be surely to become a transgressor. Far from the abandoning of the law making Christ a minister of sin, the other conclusion is the right and only one. To seek to rear anew a legal structure on which to base one's justification would indeed be to make oneself a law-breaker. Paul is giving reason for his blank, 'Certainly not!'

which he has just pronounced against the suggestion that Christ is a minister of sin. The word 'again' is therefore significant. Peter had, by his action among the Gentile believers at Antioch, reverted to the idea that law was somehow important for a man's standing before God. For Paul, any such notion was a rebuilding of what had been broken down, namely, that works of the law count in God's declaration of man's acceptance of him. If I adopt the law, Paul retorts, far from assuring me justification, it only 'proves', 'shows myself up as' (NEB), one who deliberately 'sidesteps' law's full demands (cf. 3. 10). This is the situation that results from seeking to build again what the proclamation of the faith-way has 'torn down'. This fact of the law's inability to justify and of the law's identification of the transgressor, Paul vindicates by reference to his own experience and that of the Galatians.

(ii) Justification by Works Denied

(a) The apostle's own experience is proof that the Law cannot justify 2. 19–21.

v. 19   For I through the law died to the law, that I might live to God.

There is a change from the 'we' of the previous verse to 'I'. It was the law which showed Paul how helpless and hopeless was his position. It has marked him down as a 'law-breaker' in spite of all his 'law-keeping'. But now he had become so identified with Christ that he, the-man-who-kept-the-law, counts for nothing as far as his justification is concerned. 'For' — this conjunction points back by way of reference to verses 15–18 to indicate the position into which Paul had been brought by faith in Christ Jesus, and in which he still stands. The 'I' is not meant to distinguish Paul from others, either from Peter, on the one hand, or the Gentile converts on the other. It is the 'I' of his own pre-conversion days, when, as a natural man zealous for the legal way, he sought to attain righteousness by law-keeping, only to find thereby law's defects. It was the law which brought sin to light for him (cf. Rom. 9. 13), and proved to him that he was a transgressor. It was thus he came to seek justification in another way. The real significance of his death to law, was the opening up of life to God. He said 'good-bye' to law when he said 'good morning' to Christ. It was in turning from the bondage of law that he discovered the blessing of liberty. It was the failure of the law to give life that condemned it and made him die thereto. He can respond to it no more as a way of justification. The legal way is never the life way.

By law Paul died to law: it is a startling paradox. The very law which he would fain follow turned against him. 'This law accuseth the accusing law, and condemneth the condemning law' (Luther). These are 'marvellous words, and unknown kinds of speech', according to Luther.

v. 20   I have been crucified with Christ;

Paul has died to the law; now, however, by a new turn in the metaphor of death he declares that he has been crucified, with Christ. The death of law meant his release from its legal demands as a way of justification. His crucifixion with Christ meant the annihilation of sin's burden and guilt and thus assures the reality of justification. In the Greek text, Christ is placed at the beginning of the passage. To be alive to God, is found and focused in Him; but found and focused in the reality of His death, by participation in His crucifixion. What He did on the cross He did *for* me, and in some profound sense I did in Him. In His death man had a share. By union with Him in faith and fellowship I become blended with Him in His atoning act. Believers, by virtue of their corporate belonging to Christ, were 'summed up' in His historic death; but this is subjectively ʳealized by faith (cf. v. 16; 3. 25; Rom. 6. 26 etc.).

ˀ no longer I who live, but Christ who lives in me;

AV translation is not accurate when it introduces, 'Never-ˢˢ I live'. Paul wishes rather to carry through the thought of ˀ and 'crucifixion'. Under the law there was very much of ⁱn Paul's activity. There was *effort* and *self*-justification; a to attain *self*-righteousness. But now he is dead to law ˀing crucified with Christ. Thus the life that is presently his cannot be really his but Christ's who lives in him. No longer is Paul the natural, separate, self-justifying and self-righteous man alive. He has become dead in Christ's death to all that; and is not living as an 'I' any longer but by the indwelling presence of the living Christ.

and the life I now live in the flesh I live by faith in the Son of God,

Paul has died, having being crucified with Christ, but he still goes on living. Yet he lives not as an independent 'I', but in the dependence of faith in the Son of God. In so far as he lives 'in the flesh' it is a faith life that he is living. His 'old man', that natural life of his, zealous as it was for a righteousness of its own manufacture, was there on the cross. True life unto God is his, here and now, in the sphere of human existence, by faith in the Son of God. He lives 'in the flesh', yet he lives 'in faith'. By introducing the title Son of God, Paul is accentuating something of the spiritual nature of this faith-life which is his now in the flesh. A faith, directed and located there, will assure to the believer the status of sonship in His Sonship and bring to the believer the quality of spirituality in His Godhead. Faith in the Son of God directs attention either to the objective source or to the subjective experience. If taken as an objective genitive, then attention is fixed on Christ as the Object of faith. If it is read as the 'mystic genitive', then Paul is stressing the condition of faith. It is in the relation of union with Christ that faith in the Son of God is brought about. It is in that sphere the faith-life is lived in the contemporary setting.

who loved me and gave himself for me.

Paul is expressing here in vivid and thrilling tones the fact of his own personal appropriation of all that the Son of God had done for him. The Son of God — 'for me'; that was for Paul, the always indescribable and the almost incredible wonder. 'For me' — for me Paul, and yet for any 'me' and every, this Son of God loved and gave Himself up on behalf of, and as a substitute for. Both verbs are in the aorist tense pointing back to the historical fact of Calvary. It was out of the love which was His that He gave Himself in voluntary self-surrender to the cross. This is the fact upon which faith lays hold — faith in the divine, atoning, love-act of Christ. In that faith in the Son of God there is justification; and in that faith Christ lives in me. Thus did Paul know in faith that He who was 'for me', is now 'in me'. That is Paul's glowing and grateful testimony. The 'me' of the passage is weighted with significance; 'Read therefore with great vehemency these words "me" and "for me" that thou with sure faith mayest conceive and print this "me" in thy heart, and apply it unto thyself, not doubting but that thou art of the number of whom this "me" belongeth' (Luther).

v. 21   I do not nullify the grace of God;

Did Paul pause at the end of verse 20 to allow his spirit to soar and his heart to throb? Perhaps. Now, however, he comes back to add an abrupt word by way of a retort to those who apparently had suggested that his doctrine of justification apart from the works of the law was somehow minimizing the grace of God to Israel. Or, there may even be a glance over his shoulder to Peter. To whomsoever it was, Paul flings out his strong word, 'I do not set at nought the grace of God.' Those who think so should pay attention to what I have said; those who think so have no understanding of the gospel of the cross.

for if justification were through the law, then Christ died to no purpose.

Paul's word rendered justification is the word for 'righteousness'; if such were gained through legal works, then would Christ's dying have been purposeless, and 'for nothing' (NEB). If, Paul is implying, I were really to allow the law as a means of attaining righteousness, then I would certainly be nullifying the grace of God by making the cross of Christ of none effect. But whatever others do — I, Paul, will not do so; not I. Never.

The whole section, beginning at chapter 2. 16 and running wn to 3. 5, is concerned with the topic, the way of faith. Paul been dealing with the subject as a general fact of which he elf is a special illustration. We have noted the change from n 2. 17 to that of 'I' in verse 18. In chapter 3. 1–5 Paul es the theme by reference to the Galatians themselves;

they are reminded that they found acceptance with God by faith. The 'I', therefore, of the previous section, gives place to the 'you' of this one.

(b) The Galatians' own experience is proof that the Law cannot justify 3. 1-5.

v. 1   *O foolish Galatians! Who has bewitched you, before whose eyes Jesus Christ was publicly portrayed as crucified?*

He has just said that Christ's death was 'for him'; now he recalls to the Galatians that he had proclaimed that it was no less for them. But could Christ's death be in vain? Only for them who had become fatally bewitched. To such the cross would be in truth a senseless thing, a needless tragedy. It is the situation in Galatia which Paul now takes up again from where he left off at 1. 9. 'O foolish Galatians!' Paul exclaims, as the thought of their wavering comes back to him. The term is not, however, specially one of reproach. There was no lack of intellectual sharpness among them; but what was at a minimum was spiritual sight. They were 'slow of heart' (same word as in Lk. 24. 15) to keep faith in what had been so clearly put to them. Who can it be, Paul asks, who has fascinated you with a be-witching spell? And the 'you' is emphatic; above all, *you* Galatians, among whom I laboured so much and who received me so well — that *you* should be dazed and dazzled by this false teacher is beyond words. You must have lost your wits by this bewitching.

The word for 'bewitch' had an origin in sorcery. But the apostle is not giving his approval to such magical arts because of this etymology of the term. Some ill-wisher it was who had worked his evil spell upon them by turning their eyes away from the cross. Paul had put Christ as crucified before them — before their very eyes. And how appropriate was the reference to 'eyes'. The fatal fascination which had bewitched them had cast an overshadowing darkness upon them so that their spiritual eyesight was no longer keen. Had they kept their eyes on the cross they would not have been overcome by 'the evil eye'.

And Paul had put before their eyes Christ as crucified in the clearest and boldest way. He had indeed 'placarded' it before them. Paul's word was in common use to describe public notices and proclamations. As on a notice board written in large capitals so that none could miss it, Paul had set before their eyes Christ as crucified. Even those of weakest sight, those of dullest spiritual perception, could not have failed to behold it. Thus was Christ 'publicly portrayed'. Had they only kept their eyes there they would not have been charmed away. Vividly and graphically, Paul had exhibited to the Galatians the crucified Saviour: and to Him they had looked and found life eternal.

v. 2 Let me ask you only this: Did you receive the Spirit by works of the law, or by hearing with faith?

This is a direct appeal to those Galatians to go back to the beginnings of grace in their soul. Paul the teacher now asks a question. He would 'learn' something of his converts. And he rests his whole gospel on the answer. Did the gospel justify them apart from 'law-works'? Was it not altogether of 'grace-faith'? Was it by the law or by hearing with faith? To such questions there could be only one answer. They had received the Spirit by hearing with faith. 'The law never bringeth the Holy Spirit, but only teacheth what we ought to do: therefore it justifieth not. But the gospel bringeth the Holy Spirit, because it teacheth what we ought to receive. Therefore the law and the gospel are two contrary doctrines' (Luther).

To receive the Spirit and to believe unto justification are evidently one and the same experience. For if any man have not the Spirit of Christ, he is no Christian (Rom. 8. 9 NEB). It is hearing, which leads on to faith, that brings the Spirit into the life. Not by works of the law was the Spirit received, but by faith. This is the first reference to the Holy Spirit in the epistle and is specially connected in this section with justification. The Spirit is given by God (3. 4) and received by faith (v. 2 cf. 3. 14). In 4. 6 He is called 'the Spirit of the Son'. In the practical section of the letter the Spirit is He by whom the Christian waits (5. 5) walks (5. 16), is led (5. 18), and has life (5. 25; cf. 6. 8).

v. 3 Are you so foolish? Having begun with the Spirit, are you now ending with the flesh?

Paul has taken it that the answer to the question of the previous verse is obvious — How did they receive the Spirit? By believing, of course. But if that is the way the Spirit is received it is not just for the beginning, but for all the way. Can they be so illogical as not to see that? The spiritual life is life in and through the Spirit: it must therefore be begun, continued and ended in the Spirit. It cannot be 'perfected', 'finished off' in the flesh. The contrasts are between 'beginning' and 'ending'; and 'Spirit' and 'flesh'. What is begun in the Spirit comes under the principle of like with like. Life begun in the Spirit cannot have its fulfilment outside the Spirit. There is no interchange between Spirit and flesh anywhere along the line. The Spirit is the divine life which is ours by faith. The flesh is human nature under the conditions of evil impulses and desires which the law has authority to command but has no power to control. Foolish is it for the Galatians to sidestep from life under the Spirit by which they are freed from the law.

v. 4 Did you experience so many things in vain? —

Paul expresses the hope that their frequent sufferings for Christ are not going to be proved useless (cf. Acts 14. 2, 3, 22). Love hopeth all things! It may have been that the Jews, and indeed the Jewish legalists, were the cause of the things they had suffered, in which case Paul's words would gain a deeper significance. They underwent tribulations for the sake of their liberty in Christ when first they came to faith. Can it be that these same Galatians should be mesmerized into going back on that stand by the very persons they had resisted unto suffering? That would be to nullify their position. That would be to put out of count the 'many' and 'great' things which they had undergone at their beginning in the way of faith. But, perhaps, all is not lost yet.

if it really is in vain.

Is there a faint hope still? The 'if yet', says Lightfoot, 'leaves a loophole for doubt'.

67

v. 5   Does he who supplies the Spirit to you and works miracles among you do so by works of the law, or by hearing with faith?

That is indeed a question for the Galatians to face. The verse is a repetition in a different form of verse 2. The 'He therefore', with which it begins, is Paul's way of referring back to what he was saying. 'He then', (that is, God — to ask again the question before I digressed) 'that supplies the Spirit to you', on what condition did He do it — works or faith? The idea conveyed by 'supplies' contains the answer. It is a compound word and implies that the supplying is a bountiful gift of grace. What the miracles were to which Paul refers, and whether they were physical or moral, we cannot say. Most translators prefer to render 'among', but it could be as the RV has it 'in' you. It may then be that Paul has in view the Spirit's incoming by faith, whose presence worked power in them. In this case, there is here no statement about outward miraculous charismatic manifestations. But even should it be to actual miraculous displays, the question is equally cogent. Came the Spirit and the miracles by the works of law or the hearing with faith? Will the foolish Galatians get the point? It is not Paul's fault if they do not. Will the eyes of their understanding be enlightened? It will not be Paul's fault if they are not.

6

THE PROOF OF FAITH

3. 6–18

At this point, Paul moves from the particular question he has
asked of the Galatian believers, How did you gain acceptance
with God? to the larger one, How is any person accepted by
God? He appeals to history, and takes Abraham as a special
case to vindicate the gospel of justification by faith. He chooses
Abraham deliberately, because, it would seem, the Galatians
were being urged by the Judaizers to undergo circumcision as
had the father of the Hebrews. The legalists were interested in
Abraham's circumcision and its relation to the covenant. Paul is
saying, Yes, take note of Abraham by all means, but consider that
which is more important and fundamental about him, his faith.
For the proof of faith Paul turns, then, to the case of Abraham.
But he will go on from there to show that far from making a man
right before God the law really involves him in the 'curse'.
And it is with the curse of the law that the gospel is concerned.

(i)   The Instance of Abraham

*v. 6   Thus Abraham 'believed God, and it was reckoned to him as
righteousness.'*

The word, 'Thus' or 'Even as' marks the beginning of a new
topic. It means, 'Why, it is as it was with Abraham' (Moffatt).
It is implied that an answer to his previous questions to the
Galatians had been given; that it is as a consequence of the
hearing with faith that they received the Holy Spirit. It was 'of

faith'; and so it was in the case of Abraham, for all the talk about his circumcision. Paul quotes the Septuagint version of Genesis 15. 6 for these Gentile readers. And the fact that he quotes, without specifying the reference, shows that the passage was well known to them, and that a scriptural word came with authority. Yet it was not Abraham's faith, merely as faith, which was reckoned to him as righteousness. It was that in which his faith reposed which was the ground of his acceptance with God. What Paul is illustrating is the principle of faith. The object and the quality of faith are not quite the same in the Old Testament as in the New. Yet Abraham's faith was faith in a promise of God which contained the promise of Christ. It is the faith-principle, as against the works-principle, which the story of Abraham makes clear. Thus Paul assures the answer to the question asked of the Galatians. God supplies the Spirit by faith without works, as in the case of Abraham, who was justified by faith without works. In the Spirit by faith the Galatians are 'reckoned as righteous'; in the promise by faith Abraham was 'reckoned as righteous'.

v. 7   So you see that it is men of faith who are the sons of Abraham.

It is correct to take the term 'know ye', not as an imperative as in the AV, but as an indicative. You perceive — 'you may take it, then' (NEB); this is an appeal to those 'foolish' Galatians to use their thinking. From the case of Abraham they may learn that the true sons of Abraham are those who rely on faith. Abraham was promised that he would be the father of a countless number; these promised sons are Abraham's sons. The declaration was annexed that the Gentiles would be blessed in him. Thus does Abraham become the father of the faithful. The 'sons of Abraham' are not of blood but of belief; not of flesh but of faith. Such, are sons, because their lives are based on and ordered by the same faith-principle as Abraham's (cf. vv. 9, 14, 15-17, 29). Here, again, Paul is not concerned to specify the object of this faith, although it is doubtless implied, but the means of man's acceptance before God. It is 'men of faith' who are brought into this position; men whose starting-point and fundamental principle is one of faith. These belong to God because they belong to faith — theirs is existence-in-faith. Yet it would not be right to let the emphasis fall exclusively on the thought of a mere reliance on faith, for, in the last analysis, the grounds of a man's justification is not reliance on faith as such, but on faith's Object, the God of all grace. They that are of faith, the believers, are Abraham's kin: faith is the criterion by which sons of Abraham are revealed.

v. 8   And the scripture, foreseeing that God would justify the Gentiles by faith,

This fact of Abraham's many 'faith-sons' was anticipated in the promise made to him. 'And the scripture, foreseeing' — this crediting of foresight to scripture is more than a mere figure of speech. The scripture is personified because the tie between God and scripture is a vital and necessary one. By means of the Spirit who inspired, the scriptures saw and set out beforehand God's divine plan for the inclusion of the Gentiles in the blessing of faith. The present tense for 'would justify' indicates that God's way of justifying by faith is an unchanging law of His moral government; and it brings out the certainty of His dealings with men and the sureness of His purposes.

preached the gospel beforehand to Abraham, saying,

The promise given to Abraham was substantially the gospel in anticipation. By his own justification by faith the content of the gospel was declared: and by the reference to 'all the nations' was its extent proclaimed. It was, then, the same gospel of faith for the Gentiles; the very gospel that had come to Galatia. Here in Lystra, Derbe and the other places, the promise to Abraham and the preaching to Paul came together. And the faith-man of the Old Testament and the faith-man of the New are found to be one in declaring the same faith-principle of man's acceptance by God.

'In you shall all the nations be blessed.'

In Abraham, as a consequence of the blessing bestowed upon him by faith, all nations shall be blessed. Galatia was witnessing the fulfilment of God's grand design. The words quoted are a fusion of two passages, Gen. 12. 3 and 18. 18, and by bringing in 'all the nations' of 18. 18 for 'all the families' of 12. 3, Paul assures that the Gentiles cannot be eliminated from this prior evangelical announcement of the gospel. In the promise made to Abraham the curse was lifted from all mankind; and with him, in the community of faith, blessing is open to the Gentiles.

v. 9   So, then, those who are men of faith are blessed with Abraham who had faith.

Here is an emphatic conclusion. So, then, those that be of faith — this is almost a synonym for 'believers', for 'Christians'. It is they who are blessed along with believing Abraham. Of these stones God has raised up children unto Abraham. And they are sons and heirs by faith, for neither their sonship nor their inheritance depend on ceremonies however religiously performed or righteously executed. Men of faith everywhere are one with Abraham who had faith. 'In Abraham we are blessed, but in what Abraham?' asks Luther. 'The believing Abraham, to wit; because if we are not in Abraham we are under a curse rather, even if we were in Abraham according to the flesh.' The reference in this quotation leads on to Paul's point in the two following verses.

(ii)   The Inability of the Law

From the proof he has given in the case of Abraham of the way of faith, Paul now goes on to show how dependence on the law means involvement in the 'curse' of the law. For unless every detail of the law is fulfilled and every ordinance kept, condemnation must follow. The conclusion must then surely be that works of law cannot justify; and this fact is confirmed by the scriptural declaration, The just shall live by faith.

v. 10   For all who rely on works of the law are under a curse;

It is the faith-principle which assures Abramic blessing. Thus, they who depend on law cannot share that blessing. The opening phrase is a strong universal assertion; 'For all' — every single one; all to a man — who follow law's cause come under law's curse. This does not mean that the 'curse' has been pronounced — yet. But it is there, threatening, in the background. The black cloud hovers above them. Always, therefore, there is a sense of apprehension. For who can render with entire exactitude and satisfaction the least of the law's demands, much less its weightier precepts? None. All then who would rely on the works of the law put themselves under the curse of the law.

for it is written, 'Cursed be every one who does not abide by all things written in the book of the law, and do them.'

This is a free translation of Deut. 27. 26. The issue raised by the quotation is clear-cut: find a way of keeping the law or else come under the curse. But there is none who has continued at all times in all the things written. And by a biblical statement, Paul knocks the bottom out of every hope to come to acceptance by God by way of law-works. Christ is, therefore, not truly presented as a mere helper of man's endeavours to keep the law: for already all are under its curse.

v. 11   Now it is evident that no man is justified before God by the law; for 'He who through faith is righteous shall live';

Paul introduces a new argument. To put the point in another way, he says: it is evident that no man is justified by the law-way. Not only, as he has just proved in the previous verse, because of man's inability to keep up to and keep up with the law's standards, but for the further reason that it is emphatically declared in scripture that through faith the righteous shall live. His readers are called upon to keep steadily before them the issue at stake. It is a question which affects their ultimate destiny for blessing or cursing. It has been shown that faith is the way of justification which involves blessing. Will justification and its attendant blessing be theirs who seek to attain them by the works of the law? They will not; they cannot: for the scriptural declaration is conclusive. Paul then quotes Habakkuk 2. 4 (cf. Rom. 1. 17). The Hebrew word used by the prophet is literally 'steadfastness', or 'faithfulness' (cf. Deut. 32. 30). Thus, what is declared in the prophet's message is that the righteous shall live in his faithfulness. In its context, Habakkuk is making the point that the waverer shall perish in times of trouble, while the faithful shall be preserved. But Paul sees behind this fidelity to the faith from which it springs. In this way, he brings out the deep evangelical note of the prophecy consistent with prophetic principles and gospel teaching. He sees there is no steadfastness in the divine purpose which has not its roots in man's attitude of trust in God; and this trust in God is the basis of man's justification. The righteous shall live by faith, for such rest their lives on faith. By referring to this passage in Habakkuk, the New Testament apostle lays hold of one of the clearest Old Testament examples in which faith is presented as the one necessary condition for redemption.

v. 12   but the law does not rest on faith,

The law does not spring out of faith. Faith is not its starting-point nor yet its characteristic principle. Paul is suggesting a contrast between the 'faith-attitude' of the previous verse and the 'law-attitude' of this. Faith makes for restfulness; the law for resentfulness. The law holds out a goal to be attained; the gospel a gift to be received. The law brings conflict; the gospel assures communion. The law is not concerned with the heart but with questions of the performance or non-performance of stated demands.

for 'He who does them shall live by them.'

This is the ruling principle of the law which Paul states by quoting Lev. 18. 5. The law requires things to be *done*, before the righteous life can be attained. Whatever its provisions, whether ceremonial or moral, all must be fully met; whoever fails in one requirement is constituted by the law as a 'transgressor', and is consequently 'cursed'. The one who sets himself to attain life by the works of law shall, as it were, be confined to them. But live as lawfully as he will, he shall never find life thereby. Justification stands on faith; and justification and life are for Paul convertible terms.

(iii) The Introduction of the Redeemer

These verses come in without introduction and bring Christ
into the tragic scene. His work relates to that 'curse' in which we
have become involved. We are in bondage to the curse of the
law; and from this Christ has bought us out. In some profound
sense He became a curse for us. He voluntarily placed Himself
under it — 'on our behalf'. Thus are we freed by a curse-
bearing death. We should not ourselves have dared to apply
such a term as a 'curse' to Christ, and there is a natural tendency, sometimes springing from a deep spiritual sensitiveness
and sometimes from a perverse intellectual superiority, to
minimize its meaning. But while care should be taken not to
extend the statement beyond its proper limits, it seems almost
impossible to exaggerate its intensity. Christ did know in awful
reality the effect of sin separating from God (cf. Mt. 27. 46).

v. 13   Christ redeemed us from the curse of the law,

There is emphasis on the word Christ; He, and only He, could
do this great thing for 'us'. The 'us' includes both Jew and
Gentile alike, for Paul, as a redeemed man, is writing to
'redeemed' Gentiles. It is in the redemption that is in Christ
Jesus that all distinctions become void. In their sinful need there
is 'no difference', and in the way of justification all are alike
pronounced righteous 'by faith'. To be redeemed is to be
ransomed, to be bought out as a slave would be from ownership
of one master to become the property of another. Here, the idea
is of redemption from law's slavery to become free men in
Christ. The idea of purchase is merged into that of deliverance;
we are ransomed to be free. In the term 'redeemed' there is the
idea of the 'cost'. Christ did not accomplish our redemption
easily and at little personal loss. Rather, it involved Him in the
infinite condescension of His incarnation and the immeasurable
suffering of His atonement. The 'curse of the law' refers back to
verses 10–12 where the idea was elaborated.

having become a curse for us —

This is a startling and strong declaration. For He became,

Himself, that very thing the law made us — a 'curse'. So identified was He with us that all we are became His, actually and literally His. The law brought us under its curse; and He brought Himself under it and made the very curse of the law His own. He became what we are in all the awful fulness of it. He experienced in Himself all the law's dark threatenings and all God's awful condemnation, by becoming Himself the object of divine wrath, as one by the law cursed by a holy reprobation. This is what He became 'for us'. This is what He undertook 'on our behalf', fully and finally. Yet He did 'on our behalf' this great thing only because, in some sense, He did it 'in our place'. He stood where we should have stood, but never could — as sinful and as a curse, and still Himself never a sinner and never accursed. In 2 Cor. 5. 21 it is stated, by this same apostle, that He became 'sin for us', but certainly not a 'sinner'; here it is stated that He became a 'curse' for us, but surely not Himself 'accursed'.

for it is written, 'Cursed be every one who hangs on a tree' —

The reference is to Deut. 21. 23. The Jews did not execute by hanging, but — and this is the point of the Old Testament passage — they did hang, by leaving exposed after death anyone they wanted branded as a criminal. Christ, by His own self-dedication, took the curse which was ours. Thus the place of hanging has become the place of healing. The apostle omits from the quotation the words 'accursed of God' which are found in both the Hebrew and the Septuagint, although there are good reasons for regarding the phrase as inaccurate. There is, however, a genuine sense in which the words (which are in brackets in the AV, although retained in the RSV) could have stood, for the Messiah was smitten of God and afflicted (Is. 53. 4). At the same time, their omission does not affect the argument, for Paul is not stressing here the truth of our guilt being laid upon Christ. He is concerned to underscore, as it were, the naked fact that by His actual hanging on a tree He was, in the eyes of the law, reckoned as cursed. And the Jews mocked Him as 'the hanged one'.

Throughout this passage, Paul is making clear the way Christ wrought redemption for us. It was in His death as 'a

cursed one'. And he shows that death of Christ to be 'for us' —
it is therefore a substitutionary death. The curse which He
became for us, however, is not an independent operative
principle. It is God's holy judgement upon man's sin which He
had to undergo instead of us. Paul does not state in specific
detail how Christ effected our reconciliation. What he does,
however, make clear is that God made the punishment, which
Christ took voluntarily upon Himself, valid for His own right
to deal with men in grace. Such a redemption which Christ
accomplished for us does not wear the character of a neat
transaction, a nicely balancing of the active and passive voice. It
comes rather with a feeling of mystery, yet, at the same time,
with a sense of adequacy, in which blend the reality and
integrity of God's holy justice and love.

*v. 14   that in Christ Jesus the blessing of Abraham might come
upon the Gentiles,*

Two results follow from this act of Christ's redeeming us from
the curse of the law. The first comes here in this part of verse 14.
Since it is 'by faith', as is proved in the case of Abraham, and
not by adherence to law, then the blessing is open to all Gentiles.
And it is 'in Christ Jesus'. This is more than saying 'by His
agency', although it is that; but it is for those linked in indissoluble union with Christ. Thus the blessing to Abraham is
not got by being *in* Israel, but by being *in* Christ.

that we might receive the promise of the Spirit through faith.

This is the second consequence of Christ's redeeming act.
The receiving of the Spirit is not the result of the blessing of
Abraham coming on the Gentiles, but of Christ having bought
us with a price. The opening of the door of faith to the Gentiles
and the bestowal of the Spirit through faith are the two results
which, however, experimentally unite in one. For to be justified
by faith is to receive the Spirit; and to receive the Spirit
through faith is to be justified. The 'we' again points beyond
Abraham's seed according to the flesh. Included in it are
'all men of faith who are Abraham's sons' (3. 6). They are
the people of the covenant who through the Spirit receive the

77

adoption of sons (4. 5, 6). 'And this liberty and gift of the Spirit we receive not by any other merit than by faith alone' (Luther).

(iv) The Illustration of the Covenant

Taking an illustration from human life, Paul seeks to prove that the gospel of God's covenant grace is not altered by the demands of law. Even a human covenant once made and sealed is sacred and binding. It cannot be set aside at will or be clogged up with new conditions. How much more does this principle hold with God's covenant!

v. 15   To give a human example, brethren: no one annuls even a man's will, or adds to it, once it has been ratified.

Paul calls upon the Galatians to consider a human analogy with a view to their understanding of the truth. In doing so he addresses them as 'brethren'. He is appealing to them here with a note of tenderness, in marked contrast with the sharpness of his tone in the earlier sections of his letter. He is asking them to give earnest attention to the matter as he brings before them an established fact of human relationships. If 'even a man's covenant' is made sure by agreed principles; more so must God's be. The word translated 'will' in our text ('covenant' AV, 'contract' Phillips, 'testimony' NEB), was in common use to convey the idea of an agreement between two parties. Ordinarily, in biblical literature, another term is used to render the Hebrew word for a covenant, with the notion of mutual agreement uppermost. In the RSV, the term translated 'will' is the same as that translated 'covenant' in verse 17 and seems to indicate a certain 'onesidedness' in the transaction, for in God's covenant He undertakes to fulfil all the conditions involved. It would seem best to keep the word 'covenant' in the present passage (but cf. Heb. 9. 15f.). A covenant must stand as agreed; and once agreed cannot be cancelled by either party, nor can 'fresh clauses be added', to translate the Greek word literally. It was this that the Judaizers were seeking to do with regard to God's covenant; this was their fundamental folly. If a human agreement is binding, how much more the divine.

v. 16 Now the promises were made to Abraham and to his offspring.

The promises are those which accompanied the covenant (cf. Gen. 12. 15f.; 17. 7, 8). The promises were 'spoken' (Gk.). They were orally declared so that faith was a firm conviction that God had spoken and that He would accomplish what He had said. Thus is faith belief in the veracity of God; an acknowledgement that God is true to Himself because He is true to His word.

It does not say, 'And to offsprings,' referring to many; but referring to one, 'And to your offspring,' which is Christ.

There are grammatical difficulties in this verse. It has been pointed out that the plural of the common Hebrew word for seed, more properly signifies 'grain' or 'crops' (cf. 1 Sam. 8. 15) and that the plural form does not occur in the Hebrew Bible in the sense of 'offsprings' required by Paul's argument. Attempts have been made to unearth such a usage in the Greek of Plato and the Chaldee Paraphrase for 'races' in Gen. 10. 18; Josh. 7. 14; Jer. 33. 24. The point of the argument does not, however, depend on whether Paul was aware of the exact grammatical terminology, but upon the rightness of his theological interpretation. He could well have brushed aside his linguistic objectors by referring to the facts of the case. Many branches of Abraham's descendants boasted in having Abraham as their father; but with One only, among the many, has God's covenant been established. To One, which is Christ, as the truly spiritual, in contrast with the many according to the flesh, was the promise made good. He, as the Representative One, embracing in Himself those identified with Him becomes then the context of the declaration. By using the name 'Christ', Paul stresses the idea of the union of believers with the promise. Had the apostle added the name 'Jesus' he would have widened the application of the term 'offspring'. But by not doing so, he would have us understand the Christ is here presented as incorporating in Himself, as the second Adam and Head of redeemed humanity, those who are His (cf. vv. 28, 29). In the passage, Paul is not allegorizing the scriptures as in 4. 22f., he is, rather, giving the spiritual meaning, where the Judaizers were only giving the natural. That is to say, he is looking at the Old Testament in the light of the gospel and unveiling its true significance from the perspective of faith. In the context of faith, the Old Testament is viewed as pointing on to the fulfilment of the promise in His one seed, even Christ: and in the context of experience the Christ who fulfils the promise is no solitary personality but One who has summed up in Himself the spiritual sons of Abraham.

It is clear from this verse that the apostle can make an easy transition from the idea of 'covenant' to that of 'promise' (cf. vv. 15, 17). The promise conveys the content of the covenant made with Abraham. 'Here', comments Luther, 'by a new name he calleth the promises of God made to Abraham, concerning Christ, that should bring the blessing upon all nations, a testament (covenant). And indeed the promise is a testament, not yet revealed, but sealed up. Now, a testament is not a law, but a donation or free gift. For heirs look not for law, exactions, or any burdens to be laid upon them by a testament, but for the inheritance confirmed thereby.'

v. 17   This is what I mean: the law, which came four hundred and thirty years afterward, does not annul a covenant previously ratified by God, so as to make the promise void.

God's covenant was made with Abraham before the law came; and as he has illustrated in verse 15, when a covenant is made 'no one maketh it void or addeth thereto'. Thus, the introduction of the law does not annul the promise. The function of the phrase, 'This is what I mean', is to confirm and clinch the argument already stated. Paul puts the issue plainly. The giving of the law 430 years after the making of the covenant cannot abrogate the promise. Paul's figure comes from Ex. 12. 40, 41. Stephen's 400 years (Acts 7. 6) is a round number following the prophetic passage about the length of the sojourn in Egypt (Gen. 15. 13). It is not necessary here to enter into the problem of chronology. The point of the number of years is to show that the covenant was established long before the introduction of the law. Its terms were long since signed and sealed. It is too late for any alteration to be made or any new provisions to be added, which would, in fact, only annul it. The very essence of the covenant is in its promise; a promise which rested on the fidelity of God. The term 'promise' brings into prominence the gratuitousness of the covenant. It is a covenant of grace containing the assurance that a seed of Abraham would be raised up, even Christ, in union with whom, all who believe are blessed in fulfilment of the promise made to Abraham the man of faith.

For 430 years God's promise stood alone without the imagined benefit of law. How unreasonable for the law-pushers to suppose that the law which was brought in after the lapse of so many years, and for quite another purpose, could affect in any way God's pledged word.

v. 18 For if the inheritance is by the law, it is no longer by promise; but God gave it to Abraham by a promise.

Standing opposed to one another are 'law' and 'promise'. And the acceptance of the one excludes the other. There is no possibility of a compromise between the two. Such a mixture would only miss the blessing of the promise. The promise stands not on law-works, and not on law-grace; but altogether on 'grace-faith'. The inheritance was assured to Abraham wholly and solely by a promise of God. It was He who 'gave' the promised inheritance as a lavishly bestowed gift ('as a free gift' NEB). By using a word which stresses the graciousness of the covenant-promise made to Abraham, Paul is, once again, denying to law-works any place in God's justification of the sinner. And no combination of promise and law, of grace and works, can be entertained. They just do not mix.

7

THE SUPERIORITY OF FAITH

3. 19—4. 20

Paul has shown the law and promise are opposed. There is no mean to be found between them. The coming of the law so long after the promise only serves to prove the superiority of the latter over the former. The promise of the covenant makes clear that the faith-way, a faith built upon God's own declared word, is, from the first, God's intended method in bringing man to Himself in redemption. But the question is inevitable: What purpose then did the law serve? Paul answers that the law came 'because of transgression'; that it has but a temporary significance 'until the seed came'; that it was given mediately through angels, and not immediately by God like the Gospel promise; and that it showed up the necessity for a righteousness bestowed through faith. These facts indicate the essential difference between the two ways, the bondage which the law-way brings and the blessing which the faith-way gives. Consequently, to renounce the faith-way must be unthinkable. Yet this is what the Galatians are in danger of doing. They must be reminded of the blessedness which came to them in the gospel of which the Judaizers would fain rob them.

(i) The Law and the Gospel

v. 19   Why then the law? It was added because of transgressions,

The objector comes up with his question. If the faith-way is so antithetical to the law, what significance then has the law? Paul does not shrink from dealing with this inescapable question. He makes clear the 'why' and the 'wherefore' of the law. The law was something 'added'; it was 'interpolated', and as such it did not interfere with the promise. It stood apart from the promise, having a different purpose. It was brought in 'because of transgression'. By the law is the knowledge of sin. It was the law which revealed existing evil as rebellion against divine authority. Thus did the added law bring to light sin's reality.

till the offspring should come to whom the promise had been made;

Yet the law had but a temporary purpose; it operated until the seed, that is, Christ should come (cf. v. 16b). The perfect tense, 'should come', points to the fact that the promise, made actual in the 'Seed', has continuing validity. The offspring, we have noted, is Christ; but Christ viewed as summing up in Himself all who obtain the blessings of the promise. Thus, by contrast, the effect of the law is temporary, while that of the promise is permanent.

and it was ordained by angels through an intermediary.

The law was furthermore transmitted by the agency of others. It came through the medium of angels (cf. Deut. 33. 2 LXX; Acts 7. 52; Heb. 2. 2). It found its spokesman in a human intermediary (AV 'mediator'); the reference is, of course, to Moses (cf. Ex. 3. 18; 32. 19). These facts about the giving of the law show it to be no perfect and direct revelation. The method of the law's promulgation by angels is taken by the writer of the Epistle to the Hebrews to indicate its inferiority to the salvation first spoken of by the Lord and accomplished in Him who is Son of God (cf. 1. 1—2. 18). The word for 'ordained' has the suggestion of something commanded. The law came in the form of divine imperatives — of things to be done. There is a certain note of harshness about the law which God 'ordained' through intermediaries. But the promise coming directly from Him is shot through with love and mercy. The thunder of the law merely accentuates the tenderness of the promise. The law comes from God; but grace comes with Him. The law demands obedience; but the gospel assures redemption.

v. 20   Now an intermediary implies more than one; but God is one.
It has been said of this verse that no other passage of scripture
has exercised more the ingenuity of commentators. Benjamin
Jowett has computed the number of interpretations to be 430; a
total which seems a bit excessive. Jowett may have carried over
into his statement the number of years alluded to in 3. 17!
Lightfoot is more modest; he gives the number to be between
250 and 300. In spite of this disheartening fact, however, the
drift of Paul's contention seems clear enough. A 'mediator' —
and the word is the same as in the previous verse — has the
character of a 'middle-man', an intermediary. Thus the very
term implies the existence of more than one party. And between
these parties, the mediator interposes his good offices to bring
them together. As already observed, the law came through the
mediation of Moses; it came only indirectly from God. But the
law so mediated did not end the estrangement between God and
the people. In the giving of God's covenant, no human mediator stood between. Thus the words 'but God is one' would
seem to indicate one of two things, or, maybe, both together.
In contrast with the promulgation of the law with its intermediaries, the promise came directly from God. Of the promise,
God is the one, and the only one, who originated and executes it.
He, the giver, is everything; the recipient is nothing, for such
stands before the One as a transgressor. God in the promise
acts alone. But a further and deeper note may underlie the
apostle's statement. God is One; and the One acting as the
fulfiller of the promise, the 'Seed' spoken of in verse 16, is no
mere human intermediary (cf. 4. 4f.). He, as man's representative, is one with God. Thus God is both Himself the direct
source of the promise and the only mediator of it.

v. 21   Is the law then against the promises of God? Certainly not;
The law which comes directly from God by means of other
intermediaries and the promise which rests upon God alone,
cannot be ultimately at variance. Certainly the law, as has been
shown, can neither supersede nor qualify the promise (cf. vv.
15–18). But this does not mean that they are fundamentally
contradictory. In the last issue they derive, the law indirectly

and the promise directly, from the same God; they cannot therefore operate in opposition. Both must be viewed in the light of their final purpose. The law is not 'against', 'in conflict with', the promises of God.

for if a law had been given which could make alive, then righteousness would indeed be by the law.

If, however, law and promise are not contradictory, they are in contrast. For had the law of Moses, as the Judaizers claimed, been designed to produce life which enabled men to obtain the promise, then righteousness would certainly have been due to law. Then indeed would there have been two ways of gaining the blessing of the promise, works and grace. But the fact is that the law cannot quicken: it was never designed with that intent. There is no contradiction, because law and gospel fulfil different functions. The law lays down regulations; it convicts the erring; but provision may be made, and in God's case *is* made, for the overruling of the legal verdict. The condemned man may be given a free pardon: the law does not decide that. It decides whether a man is guilty or not. The Judaizers seemed to single out from the body of law that which they took a special delight in 'adding' to the promise as a requirement necessary to be kept. But Paul, by omitting the article before 'law', here fastens attention upon the inability of any of law's provisions to be life-giving. Among all the laws of Moses not one was ordained to accomplish this end. To give life belongs alone to the life-giving Spirit.

v. 22   But the scripture consigned all things to sin,

The 'but' marks a strong contrast with what has preceded. If a law had been given which had life-giving effect, then would righteousness have been by the legal method. Such a thesis is, however, quite contrary to the actual facts as authenticated by scripture. For scripture has consigned ('imprisoned' Phillips) all things under sin. Scripture has included all under the law's condemnation. The scripture referred to as proof may be the whole tenor of the Old Testament, or, what seems more probable here, some particular passage. In the latter case it may be Psalm 143. 2 (quoted in 2. 16); or Deut. 27. 26 (quoted in 3. 10) that was in the apostle's mind. The pregnant expression rendered 'consigned all things to sin' is very emphatic. It means to shut up (cf. Rom. 11. 32), without any way of escape from the lordship of sin. It is to be 'imprisoned' by it and not to be able to break out. The 'all' is in the neuter — 'all things'. That makes the declaration all the more comprehensive: all without a single exception — 'not even in favour of the Virgin Mary' (Schaff).

that what was promised to faith in Jesus Christ might be given to those who believe.

The way of faith has already been established. So the promise which is by faith is theirs who have faith. To such alone does its blessing come; but not to those who think to obtain it through the works of the law. For all have been shut up under sin. Yet shut-up men can be let out; and that is the promise of faith to be possessed through faith. And as such it is something given not gained. 'The content of the promise flows out of the faith in Christ. Faith constitutes the connection with the source out of which issues the gift of salvation. That source is Christ. All emphasis falls on that' (Ridderbos).

v. 23 Now before faith came, we were confined under the law, kept under restraint until faith should be revealed.

Until faith came we were held in custody by law. We were under lock and key, for the law had no power to release until presented with the title deeds of pardon. There is some discussion as to the precise significance of the term 'faith' in the passage. Some read the use of the article preceding to mean, before 'The Faith' came we were held under law. Now, since the faith-way has been revealed by the revelation of Jesus Christ the only possible attitude for justification in righteousness is 'by faith'. Others prefer to push back the application further by noting that it was Paul's argument that the faith-principle had its vindication in the case of Abraham. For this reason faith is regarded subjectively as trust in the delivering grace of God. Faith and law are then personified and the interpretation given:

law always held man under its guard until faith, as believing in the promise of God, arrived with the deed of release and pardon. Lightfoot thinks that the two extremes of faith merge, the subjective, as the state of the Christian, and the objective, as the teaching of the gospel. It would seem that what Paul wishes to be understood is that law fulfilled its purpose by holding man in custody from which a righteousness assuring deliverance could only come by faith, as is proved by the story of Abraham. Now that the gospel of faith has come and is proclaimed in the Faith of the Gospel, displaying openly the title deeds of pardon to all who believe, the restraint of law is over for all. This is freedom in faith. Thus the law gives way to the gospel, both historically and experimentally, and its power to confine and its purpose to restrain are over.

v. 24   So that the law was our custodian until Christ came,

The law is then not quite useless. It acted as our 'custodian until Christ came'. The law took man into its disciplinary protection by way of preparation for the liberty which becomes actualized in Christ. Paul's term translated 'custodian', occurs frequently in Classical Greek for 'schoolmaster' or 'tutor'. But such a 'pedagogue' was usually a slave employed to act in a disciplinary and protective capacity over a boy until he reached the age of maturity. He was a sort of 'child caretaker'. The AV translation 'schoolmaster' gives the occupation too high a status. And it conveys the notion of law as a system of primary education from which man could naturally graduate to the more advanced system of the gospel. But Paul is not intending to convey the idea that the law fulfilled the pedagogue's duty by leading the child into the school of Christ. The idea of the gospel as something learned as well as something earned was foreign to Paul's teaching. For the apostle, Christ is the Redeemer, not the Teacher. He does not conceive of the Christian faith as a course in advanced religious education. It is a reception of life, a deliverance from death, a release from prison. 'The law is not a schoolmaster to bring us to another law-giver who requireth of us works, but unto Christ our justifier and Saviour' (Luther).

that we might be justified by faith.

This is the end to which the law can conduct us. But there it must leave us. It cannot give life and righteousness. The law is not opposed to the gospel; its highest value is to act as custodian, so that we may be justified by faith. But if the law shuts us up to sin, the gospel shuts us off from law.

v. 25   But now that faith has come, we are no longer under a custodian;

The period of tutelage is over: we are out of our minority — we are now in faith, 'full grown sons'. Thus the law is only opposed to the gospel when we stay in it after grace has come. In faith we are 'now', 'no longer' what we once were. The period of law is passed and gone — we are not under the law but under grace. The custodian has withdrawn; the schoolmaster has stepped aside.

v. 26   for in Christ Jesus you are all sons of God, through faith.

Note should be taken of the change from the 'we are' of the previous verse to the 'you are' of this one. There is a transition from argument to appeal. By returning to law the Galatians were going back to custody; they would be forfeiting the dignity of sonship. You are sons, all of you, by union with Christ — Paul's veiled appeal is; Be what you are. You are 'in Christ' by being 'in faith', and therein lies your relationship of sonship.

v. 27   For as many of you as were baptized into Christ have put on Christ.

This verse contains the only reference to baptism in the letter. And it is made the basis of an argumentative appeal as it is in Romans (cf. ch. 6). Just as the Roman youth put on his toga, so in baptism had they put on Christ. The 'baptism into Christ' refers back to 'faith in Christ' on verse 26. In both, there is a conscious act, for the Greek verb about their baptism is in the middle voice, so as to express the fact that they had themselves baptized, as they themselves had believed. Baptism indicates the position of faith against the practice of law. In baptism, they declared the faith by which they were justified. There their sonship was attested. And as they had been clothed with water as a garment in their baptism, so had they put on Christ as their robe of righteousness. They had taken to themselves the character of Christ the Righteous One. Thus they had received their standing in His standing, and their sonship in His Sonship. And having declared their acceptance 'in faith' — how could they be induced to believe that works were no longer necessary? The phrase 'as many of you as were baptized' brings out the indiscriminate nature of grace. The expression 'as many' is co-extensive with the 'you are all' of verse 26. Thus baptism becomes itself a sort of evidence of the nature of grace. Both Jew and Gentile alike 'put on Christ' in baptism and so declare that they share equally in the grace of Christ.

The baptism is stated to be 'in' or 'into' (Phillips) Christ. But there is no mystical or mechanical notion in Paul's view. 'What happens at baptism is a confirmation and sealing, a visible manifestation of what is given to the church by faith. So much is true, however, that Paul wants to indicate by his objective-sacramental mode of expression, and by appealing especially to baptism for establishing the sonship of believers, that the reality of becoming one with Christ is nowhere so clearly revealed or so firmly founded in the Christian consciousness of faith as in this baptism (cf. Rom. 6. 3ff. and Col. 2. 12ff.)' (Ridderbos).

v. 28   There is neither Jew nor Greek, there is neither slave nor free, there is neither male nor female;

In the light of the faith they have declared in baptism, 'there is no room for' any apartheid. Every wall has tumbled; all barriers have been swept away. No particular claim can be entered; no special disabilities can debar, because none exist any longer. All partitions are levelled. Curtains have been pulled aside; borders have been made to cease; frontiers between nation and nation; segregation of colour from colour — all have gone. Jew and Greek; there go racial distinctions — the black and the white; the national and the immigrant. Slave and free; there go social distinctions — the capitalist and the labourer; the affluent and the underprivileged. Male and female; there go sex differences — the man and the woman; the boy and the girl.

for you are all one in Christ Jesus.

There is where all become one — in Christ Jesus. All are 'one man' (masculine) in Him. There they are on the s me level. There is no special class in grace. Sin levels all men to the same low position; grace lifts all men to the same high privilege. Sin puts us under the table as slaves; grace puts us at the table as sons. And all the seats are of equal status. But there is a double edge to Paul's statement: for not only are all one who are 'in Him', but also all who are 'in Him' are one. They are not only on the same platform, but they are also one personality by a vital union with Christ. Both ideas are stated by Paul elsewhere (cf. I Cor. 3. 8; 10. 17; 12. 12, 13; Col. 3. 15).

v. 29   And if you are Christ's, then you are Abraham's offspring,

If you are Christ's — if you have faith in Him and have put on Christ, then, Gentiles though you are, you are Abraham's seed. You are of Abraham's family, even if you are not of Abraham's nation. The genitive (Christ's) denotes a relationship of intimacy — if you are one with Christ, identified with Him, then you are one with Abraham's seed. Then you are identified with Abraham's offspring.

heirs according to promise.

This is the peak of the promise. Heirs, but not of Abraham according to the flesh. Heirs of God, because the promised inheritance has become ours by faith (cf. Rom. 8. 16, 17). By union with Christ, the believer, whether Jew or Gentile, slave or free; male or female, is constituted the true spiritual son of Abraham, and secures all the blessings promised by faith as against all strivings to gain the inheritance by works of the law. There is no article in the Greek before the word 'promise', for the apostle is not thinking, either here or in verse 18, so much about the terms of the promise as about its character as God's gift of grace.

(ii) The Slave and the Son

v. 1 *I mean that the heir, as long as he is a child, is no better than a slave, though he is the owner of all the estate;*

The beginning of chapter 4 does not signal a real break in the thought. Paul continues the subject by illustrating his thesis with reference to the relationship between the slave and the son. Since Christ has come we have attained our freedom as sons. We have been redeemed from under the law and know in our hearts the spirit of sonship. 'Now I say', says Paul, using a phrase by which he would signify that he is about to explain and elucidate what he has affirmed. As a 'child' the heir has not entered upon his privileged responsibilities as 'owner of all the estate'. The child is but 'a minor', and as such is still under tutelage. He has still the immaturity of youth as well as the incapacity of childhood. *De jure* he may be lord of all, but he is treated as a household slave. He cannot act in freedom for he has not come to his rights. Being in infancy, the heir cannot be reckoned as a grown man. The apostle, however, does not appear to be stating a technical legal expression by his use of the term 'child'. But the idea is clear; the heir, until he has reached the time of understanding, is limited from coming into the enjoyment of what is his 'by promise'.

v. 2 *but he is under guardians and trustees until the date set by the father.*

The guardians control his person and the trustees his property. From the first to last he is in the control of others. The words for 'guardians' and 'trustees' are rightly translated as plurals, for Paul would show how complete and comprehensive is the authority under which the child lives. He is in subjection to the powers appointed over him. His condition is one of abject slavery. Yet something of a change is foreshadowed. For the father fixes the time when the heir apparent becomes the apparent heir. In Roman law that time was decreed by statute but with the father's general consent. The father appears to have had some part in the ordinance. But Paul seems to want to imply that in His dealings with men it is God alone, as Lord of time, who set the day of His own appointment (cf. v. 4).

v. 3 So with us; when we were children, we were slaves to the elemental spirits of the universe.

As in the case of the child, although an heir, yet a slave, so is it with us. Paul may have had in mind by this 'us', the Jewish Christians, in particular, of whom he was one. But what he says is equally applicable to all believers, whether Jews or Gentiles as descriptive of their pre-Christian days. For all who were not under the tutelage of the Mosaic law were 'slaves to the elemental spirits of the universe'. Everyone has his period of childhood, when hoping to inherit eternal life they seek to have it by some act of their own by which to merit it. They find themselves then held in bondage.

The word rendered in the RSV and NEB by the phrase 'elemental spirits' is the one plural word in the Greek — *stoicheia*. The limiting term 'spirits' has been added by the translators. Originally, the term signified stakes set out in rows, either to mark off a boundary or to hang nets upon. From this developed the idea of the letters of the alphabet placed side by side, thus connoting the basic constituents of human speech. Two possibilities are then open for an understanding of what the apostle means. First, there is the physical use, to signify those elements which constitute the material structure of the universe, as earth, air, fire and water (cf. 2 Pet. 3. 10–12). Second, the religious use, to refer to those rudimentary ideas of a non-Christian character which constitute the alphabet, so to speak, of the human race, and the system of rites and ceremonies which serve as the picture-book lessons of childhood (cf. Col. 3. 8, 20 where the 'rudiments of the world' are associated with 'the traditions of men' — the philosophy of vain deceits). But whether these elements are considered to be childish teachings or tyrannizing spirits is not possible to determine. Or did Paul leave it vague on purpose? What a blow to the Judaizers to be told that their traditions and systems were like the picture-books of children! And what a shock for the Gentiles to learn that what they had left behind when they came to faith in Christ were the primitive fears of the natural man! For either of them to want to put themselves back under the conditions of childhood and slavery must seem incredible. Herein is revealed the superiority of the Christian gospel; it delivers alike from the fear of law and from the law of fear. Both Jewish ritual and Gentile religion are but rudimentary, fit for children and slaves; for the slave condition of children and the child condition of slaves.

v. 4   But when the time had fully come,

This is one of the decisive 'buts' of scripture. It marks a new epoch, a new beginning, the start of a new chapter. The fulness of time is, of course, the time appointed by the Father (cf. v. 2). It was the moment of God's ordaining — His occasion and ours, for it was with man in view that the time was set. God always keeps His appointments — He is not slack concerning His promises. He does not hurry to fulfil His plan nor does He fall behind. It was just at the right time He acted; the time divinely fixed and historically fitting. It was just when the pedagogic position of the law could be understood for what it was. It was from all points of view, even when seen from the historical and psychological perspective, manifestly God's occasion. The tragic inability of man under the law was now fully realized and the full scope of sin revealed. What was to come about was accomplished, and the condition into which man had brought himself set the stage for God's event, for God's happening. All was ready; all was right.

God sent forth his Son,

When the time was 'fully come' God sent forth. The time came about, but He did not then come to be. God 'sent forth' 'his Son'. And He was there to be sent forth; there in the reality of His pre-existence and there in the uniqueness of His relationship. For He had His being there, as Son. It was such a One who was commissioned to accomplish the divine intention when the time had fully come (cf. 1 Cor. 8. 6; Phil 2. 6f.; Col. 1. 15f.).

born of woman, born under the law,

This declaration concerns the fact of the presence in human

93

nature of God's Son. Here we have in brief statement the history of our Lord who is the Lord of history. He came 'born of woman' He took upon Himself our human condition. Paul is concerned to stress the fact rather than to indicate the method. The AV has 'made of a woman', and there is something to be said for that translation (cf. 3. 13; Jn. 1. 14, etc.). If it could be sustained as undoubted here, then it would seem that Paul is making some allusion to the supernatural mode of His entry upon the human scene. It is, however, more plainly the reality of His being 'sent forth', than the way of His coming, that is in the apostle's mind. He came both born of woman and born under law. The word for 'born' is the same in each place. He was 'born under the jurisdiction of the Law' (Phillips). It was 'under the law as a legal system' that He came to live His life in the flesh. He subjected Himself to all its requirements, circumcision included. And did not His fulfilling of the law only go to show how impossible it is for the law to be fulfilled? By being 'born of a woman' He assumed humanity, and came under the law's conditioning by taking its yoke upon Himself.

v. 5 *to redeem those who were under the law,*

By using the term 'redeem', which has to do with the method of delivering slaves, Paul was alluding again to the fact of the imprisoning power of the law. How Christ accomplished this deliverance has already been stated (cf. 3. 13). He was brought under the law that we might be brought from under it. The term here is, however, not restrictive. Of course Paul has most obviously in mind the law as legalistically understood. But even the law of conscience (cf. Rom. 1. 19f.; 2. 20f.) condemning to guilt the Gentiles is here implied. Explicitly then was the Son of God 'sent forth' to liberate man from any and every system by which he is condemned and held bondage. This is His work to accomplish — a work that only He could do, both Godlike and Divine.

so that we might receive adoption as sons.

This is the second grand result of His coming upon the stage of human history. The word for 'in order that' comes twice. He took our humanity and the yoke of law (i) to redeem and (ii) to adopt. The first sets our sights more on the objective fact. For the whole drama of His pre-existent glory, His entry into human life, His earthly ministry, His death and resurrection are implied in His being born of woman and under the law in order that redemption might become a historic fact. To receive the adoption as sons is a consequence of the redemption; it is indeed what constitutes it subjectively 'in our hearts' by the indwelling Spirit. Ours is a sonship of adoption. It is a gift of grace. Christ is God's Son without qualification, without question. Ours is a sonship which is open to faith; an adoption which 'we might receive'. The 'we' here indicates the universality of this installation as sons; this does not mean that every person becomes 'naturally' a son of God: all without distinction may become so, but not all without exception. For the adoption is 'received' by faith; it is not merited by works or mediated by ceremonies. The phrase 'adopted as sons' is all-inclusive indeed but it has its experimental beginning in the inner witness of the Spirit (cf. 4. 6; Rom. 8. 14, 15), and its experimental consummation when as 'heir' we enter into full and final fellowship with God (cf. 5. 7; 1 Cor. 15. 24f.).

v. 6   And because you are sons, God has sent the Spirit of his Son into our hearts, crying, 'Abba! Father!'

Once again, Paul makes an appeal to the experience of the Galatians; so note the 'you' (cf. 3. 2f.). Their reception into sonship is here regarded as antecedent to the Spirits presence. But this must not be taken to mean that a different experience is to be sought for the two. Paul is concerned in the passage to express the fact of the believers' adoption as sons in the redeeming work of God's Son. And to that adoption the Spirit is the inner witness. It is, therefore, proper to the context to see here the imparting of the Spirit as bringing into vivid awareness this adoption as sons. Sometimes the apostle, as here, makes the sonship of believers the ground of their receiving the Spirit; at other times the presence of the Spirit is made the means of the believers' sonship (cf. Rom. 8. 15 NEB). There is no real contradiction, but rather the proof of the reciprocity of the gift of sonship and of the Spirit. As the Son was 'sent forth' to redeem unto adoption, so now it can be said that the Spirit is 'sent forth' (same word) to authenticate unto sonship (cf. Eph. 1. 13). And significantly, the statement concerns 'the Spirit of his Son'. This is the only place where the Holy Spirit is so described. But it is very relevant in the context which relates to sonship. It is the same Spirit who prompted Christ's actual sonship in the days of His flesh, who does likewise for the believers' adopted sonship. And by Him we are able to voice our sonship since He cries within our hearts — the very innermost sanctuary of our being — 'Abba, Father'. It is the joyous recognition of God as Father which is the distinguishing mark of the Spirit's presence. The Spirit operates 'in our hearts', whereas the law moves in the sphere of the external. The Spirit gets to the very heart of the matter because by Him we are directed to the matters of the heart.

v. 7   So through God you are no longer a slave but a son,

'So' — because of the fact that the Father has sent forth His Son to redeem us unto adoption and because of the Spirit's witness to our sonship by the Father, 'through God' — through the Triune God, Father, Son and Spirit, it then must be that our slavery has gone and our sonship has begun.

and if a son then an heir.

As an heir, all the promises are now realized. The childhood days are over. The thought of heirship has been in Paul's mind (cf. 3. 18, 29). He returns to it here by way of a reminder to the Galatians that it was not by law, but by their new standing of freedom in Christ by faith that the blessings promised to Abraham were theirs. Into that position they were brought by the gospel. Would they, could they, now turn back?

In the light of this sonship and heirship it is unthinkable surely to return to bondage. Paul has presented a reasoned argument to preclude it. With the same end in view, he now comes in with an eager expostulation. When they were ignorant of God then they were in bondage to what were no gods (cf. 1 Cor. 10. 20). But now they are known of God, the true God revealed in Christ. There can be no excuse for desiring to revert to slavery.

v. 8   Formerly, when you did not know God,

The passage begins with a 'But' which marks an antithesis. How different they were 'at one time' from the position they now enjoy (cf. vv. 7, 9). Paul often took occasion to contrast the state of the Gentile believers in their former paganism with the status accorded to them in the faith of the gospel (cf. Rom. 11. 17–25; 15. 8, 9; 1 Cor. 12. 2; Eph. 2. 11–17). Here, however, his words come with indignant passion in view of the situation developing in Galatia. What Paul wants to convey is that the thought of reverting to their former condition is tantamount to a renouncing of the knowledge of the one true God they had come to know. Formerly, they were ignorant of Him.

The apostle always regarded it as an integral part of His gospel to declare the Godhood of God. Not that he needed to prove 'that God is'; he could begin with the presupposition of a belief in the existence of a Divine reality (cf. Acts 17. 23). But the ignorance had reference to 'what God is': and what God is he had learned by the revelation given to him. It had come to clear focus only in Christ, God's Son. So Paul constantly affirms that Gentile paganism was ignorant of God's true nature. 'Knowing not God' is for him a summary characterization of the pre-Christian state of Gentiles (cf. 1 Thess. 4. 5; 2 Thess. 1, 8 etc.). Such was the condition of the Galatians in the 'when' of their past ignorance.

you were in bondage to beings that by nature are no gods;

This is the result of their not knowing God and, maybe, a partial excuse for that condition. It was ignorance of God which enmeshed them in slavish servitude (the aorist tense denotes that this was their former state as a whole) to beings which have no divine status. Not that the objects of their worship were non-existents, but that rather they were such creatures that were not of the nature of God. These beings, 'elemental spirits' it may be, (cf. v. 3), were real enough to the Gentile world; but none-theless their divine being was not real.

v. 9   but now that you have come to know God, or rather to be known by God,

The 'now' of this verse contrasts with the 'then' of the previous one. It marks the fact that the 'former' condition is theirs no longer. Old things have passed away. A new relationship is theirs — sons; a new position is theirs — heirs. It is, therefore, against the background of verses 6 and 7 that this statement must be read. Now they know God, and knowing Him they are no longer ignorant. They now know Him of whom they were previously without knowledge; they know Him as God and in so acknowledging His absolute Godhood they deny godhood to the beings they once served in slavish ignorance.

But Paul adds immediately, 'rather to be known by God'. He makes this change lest there should be any lingering idea that their reconciliation by the knowledge of God was through any effort of their own. Some would regard the use of 'known' in this verse as suggesting an intimate and personal knowledge of God — a knowledge of acquaintanceship rather than a knowledge of mere existence. Thus to know God in this way is not of man's devising and discerning. It is a knowledge imparted. It is a knowledge of God which comes in the God-given awareness of being the object of His grace (cf. Rom. 9. 25f; 11. 30; 1 Cor. 8. 3, etc.). 'This is a true knowledge of God, and a divine persuasion, which deceiveth us not' (Luther).

The verse is an illustration of a Pauline amended expression. Paul was almost too fluent in his use of words; they sometimes got ahead of his thoughts and only when he was half-way through did he realize where he was going. The entrance of the 'rather' of self-correction is a feature of his writings. 'It is Christ that died, yea rather —'; 'But now you have come to know God, or rather —'. Yet, of course, Paul is not really correcting himself except by enlargement: 'It is Christ that died' — Yes indeed, but more — 'yea, rather that is risen from the dead'. 'But now that you have come to know God' — but no, not quite that — 'or rather to be known by God'.

how can you turn back again to the weak and beggarly elemental spirits, whose slaves you want to be once more?

How pertinent is that question! Never having known God and being in bondage is bad enough, but to have come to be known of God and then to seek once more the bondage from which they have been delivered is beyond understanding. To meddle again with the ABC of the child's picture-book, when they could be exploring all the rich life-literature of the faith, is surely to become weak and a return to slavery. The verse is in the form of a rhetorical question to denote the absurdity of the whole notion. Yet the present tense suggests that what seems beyond the bounds of possibility has already begun. The Galatians had taken some steps back to the futile and fruitless system of their former state, and were leaving behind the rich and real blessings into which they had been brought by the gospel of faith. 'And therefore every man that revolteth from the knowledge of Christ, must needs fall into idolatry, and conceive such a notion of God, as is not agreeable to His nature' (Luther).

v. 10   You observe days, and months, and seasons, and years!

They observe, but they are not observant. They keep all the rituals enforced upon them by the Judaizers, but fail to keep all the riches assured to them in the gospel. They were being strangled in their set times; their sabbath keeping, their new-moon celebrations, their annual festivals. And what they did they did with religious scrupulosity, for the word Paul uses for 'observe' is a compound which means, literally, 'you go along with and observe' (cf. Ps. 129. 3). It is all done exactly as required — all to the final minutia and to the fullest measure. But the more they try out the rules, the more they are tied up in them. So were the Galatians being led along adroitly by the Judaizers. The ritualists had not yet got them to the place of accepting all they required of them. But they had them on the way. First the round of feasts and fasts, then circumcision; and, what next? Paul knew well what that would be; a religion drained of all reality, a message robbed of all mercy. How can he not but speak out of the fulness of his heart of such a situation as that.

v. 11   I am afraid I have laboured over you in vain.

The word for bestowed labour is in the perfect indicative mood because the apostle suspects that the mischief he fears has already taken place. Thus does Paul give vent to his feelings regarding the tragedy of the position into which the Galatians were moving. To see his labour so easily lost, and his toil terminated so fruitlessly, is more than even an apostle can stand; more by far than he can take silently. For, if what had begun among the Galatians were to go on unhindered, and reach its full outworking, all he had sought to do would indeed be for nothing. For the apostle it would mean the sorrow of a great disappointment; and for the Galatians it would be shipwreck by a spiritual disaster.

In this section it is striking to observe how Paul equates the Jewish position under the law with the heathen position under superstition. In some important respects, there must, of course, be vast differences between the two. But one principle underlies them both. 'Doth Paul take it to be one thing, to fall from the promise to the law, from faith to works, and to do service to them which by nature are no gods?' asks Luther. He replies to his own question, 'I answer, whosoever is fallen from the article of justification is ignorant of God, and is an idolater. Therefore it is all one thing, whether he turn against the law, or to the worshipping of idols . . . The reason is, because God will or can be known not otherwise than by Christ . . . There is no mean betwixt man's work, and the knowledge of Christ . . . If this knowledge be darkened or defaced it is all one whether thou be a monk, a Turk, or a Jew'.

(iii) The Past and the Present

In the nature of a very affectionate appeal to the Galatians, in this passage Paul continues his main theme of the superiority of faith. He indicates the anguish which the estrangement from them has occasioned, and he expresses his passionate desire to get the cause of such a condition removed. He had laid aside his privileges as a Jew for their sakes. He had virtually put himself in the position of a Gentile. Can they not see the rightness of this? And can they not throw off the yoke of Judaism which they are foolishly fastening upon themselves, and be free as he is?

v. 12   Brethren, I beseech you, become as I am, for I also have become as you are.

'Be as I', that is the burden of Paul's appeal (cf. 1 Cor. 11. 1). Once Paul had been a zealous worker for a legal righteousness. But that he abandoned, when God made Himself known to him in grace for salvation. He had thus put himself on a footing with the Gentiles, as having no merit to plead. That is the place where God meets man in grace. Paul's appeal to the Gentiles is to take his line as he once took theirs. There is a deep argument in his appeal. For the fact that he has been able to cast off the trammels of the legal ceremonial shows that he regarded it as no longer contributing anything to his standing before God. The Galatians should likewise free themselves from the bondage of ordinances and be free in faith as he has become. His words to them well up out of a heart of loving sympathy as their fellow-worker in the gospel of Christ. He had become an utter outcast from Jewish sympathy. How much more should not they allow themselves to be so reckoned who, as Gentiles, were always considered such by the Jews. An imploring intensity comes in the words, 'Brethren, I beseech you'.

You did me no wrong;

It is not easy to follow Paul's thought at this point. His words may be either an oblique way of saying, 'I received nothing but kindness at your hands', or they may be meant to forestall any possible misunderstanding on the part of the Galatians that he was for some reason personally offended by them. The words seem to introduce a new sentence which runs through to verse 15. If this is so, then the latter interpretation is to be preferred. The apostle has been writing with not a little indignation. He is aware that an apprehension may have arisen in his readers' minds that he was upset, as the charge he had to make against them because of their virtual betrayal of him might suggest. Paul will re-assure them. His displeasure is not at all personal, but on account of their wavering and waning attitude to the gospel. Yet a further thought may be implied: the Galatians may have asserted that they had done no wrong to the apostle. Paul counters that that was so when first he came among them with the gospel — 'You did me no wrong, but you know that it was because of some bodily ailment that I preached the gospel'. You then received me as God's angel, even as Christ Jesus Himself. Receiving him in this way at the beginning, what has happened now, that they have hesitancy and suspicion regarding him? (cf. v. 16).

v. 13   you know it was because of a bodily ailment that I preached the gospel to you at first;

It was evidently as a result of some illness that Paul had gone to Galatia in the first instance. But in spite of what appears to have been the repulsive nature of his ailment and the compulsory nature of his coming, the Galatians had given him an enthusiastic welcome. What the particular sickness was which had necessitated the apostle's entry into the region it is not possible to say. Most commentators identify it with the 'thorn in the flesh' of 2 Cor. 12. 7. Several other suggestions have been made such as fleshy desires, spiritual trials, bodily weakness, results of persecution, bad eyesight, epilepsy. But whatever it was, it was of such a nature that might have been expected to evoke contempt from the Galatians. Instead they treated him in a most praiseworthy manner.

v. 14   and though my condition was a trial to you, you did not scorn or despise me,

Paul's infirmity could have occasioned such reaction from the Galatians. The AV locates the cause of such a possible reaction 'in my flesh'. The NEB rendering makes the suggestion that they 'resisted any temptation to show scorn or disgust at the state of my poor body'. Evidently, the apostle's condition was itself a temptation to the Galatians to 'reject' his presence among them as being a man signally favoured by God. It was a high compliment to them that they did not judge by outward appearances, but that they somehow recognized Paul as the possessor of a heavenly treasure in an earthly vessel.

but received me as an angel of God, as Christ Jesus.

Undoubtedly Paul was God's messenger. But the Galatians came speedily to regard the apostle in a higher light. For the glory of his message and the grace of his behaviour coalesced that they could not but suppose him to be worthy of such honours as becomes an unearthly visitant. The first possible temptation to dismiss and despise him was soon overcome by the Galatians. So completely was the plight of the earthen vessel lost in the splendour of the treasure which it contained that the Galatians quickly came to see that the man and his message were completely one. He who spoke to them of Christ Jesus was to them the living demonstration of the gospel he proclaimed. He embodied the grace of the gospel. He was manifestly so absorbed in the glad tidings and his whole being so irradiated with the goodness and gladness of it that the Galatians could only respond with an unbounded enthusiasm. Christ Jesus had surely come among them, living in Paul's life and alive in Paul's gospel.

v. 15   What has become of the satisfaction you felt?

In this visit of Paul, the Galatians had congratulated themselves. What gain it had been to them that he had come among them and that they had resisted the temptation to repudiate his presence. They had received the gospel of freedom from him. But now! Have they forgotten the happiness they thought themselves to possess in having him among them? They had then desired him, now they would desert him. They had regarded his coming to them as a veritable sign of heavenly goodwill. Why do they not regard him still as Christ's true man? What has become of that congratulation of themselves? What indeed?

For I bear you witness that, if possible, you would have plucked out your eyes and given them to me.

The Galatians would have done anything for Paul, who had come as Christ's very self among them. If plucking out their eyes could have benefited the apostle they would have gladly undergone the ordeal. This passage is quoted by those who contend that the ailment which sent him to Galatia was something that had gone amiss with his eyes. Could it be that the blinding experience of the Damascus road had remained with him throughout his afterlife, as a perpetual reminder that his gospel was truly 'from above'? Perhaps, however, the idea of a defect of eyesight must not be overstressed as Paul's language barely escapes hyperbole even by the use of the expression 'if you were able' rather than 'if necessary'.

v. 16   Have I then become your enemy by telling you the truth?

The question is, when did Paul deal thus honestly with the Galatians which they could construe as enmity? Some refer it to the occasion of his second visit to the area. It would seem better, however, to refer it to this letter. Paul's point then is: you once certainly did consider me a heaven-sent messenger — do not cease to think of me as anything less, because I write as I do. What he says now is what he said then; the truth has not changed. The words would seem better translated as an assertion rather than as a question ('Therefore' does not introduce a question elsewhere in the New Testament). Paul is, apparently, aware of the hostility which had developed towards him among the Galatians and he exclaims: 'Therefore I am become your enemy by telling you the truth!'. The suggestion is one of amazement. 'Frankly you stagger me' (4. 11 Phillips).

v. 17   They make much of you, but for no good purpose;

Paul once held the first place in their esteem for the gospel's sake; now he is regarded as an enemy. Others have stepped into his place, not as he had done to bring the Galatians into the freedom of Christ, but into bondage. That was their purpose. These legalist advocates zealously seek you, they pay court to you, with a view to winning you over to their side. They sought to curry favour with the Galatians, but with dishonest intent.

they want to shut you out, that you may make much of them.

So that they may be esteemed, they would shut off the Galatians from Paul's authority and message, and thus from all the privileges of the gospel and fellowship with those who hold to the doctrine of justification by faith in Christ. By gaining your favour under pretence that they are the true teachers they seek to gain all the more honour and attention. By being shut out from Christ the Galatians are shut up to them — a fatal enclosure. By being detached from Paul's teaching and made to feel that they had been led somewhat astray by him in respect of their acceptance by God, they were induced to look upon their new teachers as sympathetic advisers to whom they were indebted for their fuller understanding of the faith. Under this cover they made themselves out to be somewhat, and consequently to gain the confidence and submission of the Galatians. What they want is to bar the door to you that you may come to envy them (NEB).

v. 18 For a good purpose it is always good to be made much of, and not only when I am present with you.

This statement has caused some difficulty. Two possibilities are open: (i) Paul is suggesting that he is not grudging the Galatians the interest shown in them by others. He is well aware that he has no monopoly in this respect. It is all right that concern for them should be shown by others; but only for a good purpose. (ii) Paul is discounting any complaint on his part for the attention displayed by others to the Galatians and their warm-hearted response thereto. Such is a good thing in itself, as he could appreciate from the enthusiastic manner of his own welcome. But he implies nonetheless his disappointment that their feelings for him have grown cold during his absence. The main drift of his words appears simple enough. It is a good thing to be sought after for a good purpose — always so, whether or not Paul, the apostle, is present. 'It is a grand thing that men should be keen to win you, whether or not I'm there, provided it is for the truth' (Phillips). But there seems to underlie the declaration the contrast between the persistent seeking after the Galatians for their good and that of the Judaizers which was 'for no good purpose' (v. 17).

v. 19   My little children, with whom I am again in travail until Christ be formed in you!

The phrase, 'My little children' pulsates with tender affection. For the apostle had lost nothing of his love for the Galatians, however much they may have changed in their regard for him. But the term is more than an expression of endearment. For in a spiritual sense they were 'children' begotten by him (cf. 1 Cor. 4. 15; Philem. 10; 1 Tim. 1. 18; 2 Tim. 2. 1). They were his spiritual children, but they had produced the occasion for renewed pangs since he must 'travail again' on their account. He did that once when he brought them to Christ; now, by their relapse, the mother's pangs must be gone through yet again to the end that they may be Christians in whom Christ alone lives, and in whom alone they have life. Paul's relation to them is not merely that of courting their favour, but like that of a mother in labour with her child. By using the figure of 'travail', the apostle indicates to the Galatians the anguish he is suffering for them because of their defection. But he is ready for it, if, at the end, Christ may be 'formed' in them. The verb occurs only here in the New Testament in its uncompounded state. It is found in the fourth-century *Apostolic Constitutions* (iv. 7) where it is translated 'formed man in the womb'. So Paul would have Christ 'formed' in them. And the preposition is significant. For Christ is not presented to them as a model to which they had to conform themselves. It is rather, that Christ Himself lives within to be the One who conforms them into His own likeness (cf. 2. 22). Christ 'in you' is the theme of the letter — for the Christian life is not obedience to a legal system but the experience of the expulsive power of an indwelling Lord. Until the Galatians are so persuaded of the truth and possessed by the Christ, Paul is ready for 'travail'. 'Until' that takes place he cannot reject the toil or refuse the trouble — 'until' Christ's likeness has taken shape in them.

v. 20   I could wish to be present with you now and to change my tone,

I could wish to be present with you, links up with verse 18. If he were now among them he would most certainly change his tone. Paul regrets having to write as he does; for in so doing, he has given the impression that he has beome their enemy (cf. v. 16). The fact is, however, that his affection for the Galatians is as strong as ever (cf. v. 19). It was out of a genuine concern for them that he felt compelled to write. He was fearful lest they slip away irrevocably from the gospel they had learned from him. But what other course could he take, being absent from them? How else could he write? It hardly seemed a time for gentleness. How much Paul wished he could be there with them in the present distress; but that was beyond possibility because of distance and duty. If he were among them he would have 'changed his tone'; but his tone only, not his gospel or his position. He might in fact, have dealt with the situation with even sterner reasonings and fuller exposition and greater understanding. He cannot say: for as it is he is at his wits' end.

for I am perplexed about you.

Paul confesses himself at a loss how to deal with them. Remote from them, he is uncertain about their state of mind. But if he is perplexed, he is not in despair. He can but hope that his letter will come to them with apostolic authority and that they will hear in it the voice of the living Christ, who can be present where Paul cannot. Should that be so, then they will be brought back again on the right track. For Paul, love suffereth all things and hopeth all things; so he will suffer still and hope on.

8

THE BLESSINGS OF FAITH

4. 21–31

Paul now turns to the final argument on which is based the very
nature of the law itself. The law declares itself inferior to the
gospel and in so doing enhances the blessings which are by faith.
To make clear his point, the apostle adopts the rabbinical use of
scripture, the allegorical method. Accepting without question
the divine inspiration of the Old Testament scriptures, he takes
as allegory the birth of Abraham's two sons as 'written with
another meaning' (cf. v. 24). The two women represent the two
covenants, the law and the promise. The Judaism of the natural
Israel is the bondage typified by the bondwoman Hagar and her
son: the gospel, and the liberty it gives to believers, is presented
by the freewoman and her son. Jerusalem which is above is the
spiritual kingdom of Christ. The statement that this Jerusalem
which is above is our mother is supported by Isaiah 54. 1. There,
Sarah is the 'desolate one', while Hagar is the one taken by
Abraham into the relationship of 'the married wife'. Believers
are in the category of Isaac, having their existence in a promise
and not by any human devising. As in the earlier record, so now
it is still true that 'Ishmael' persecutes 'Isaac' but the persecution is doomed to failure, for it stands decreed that 'the
bondwoman shall not be heir with the son of the freewoman'
(v. 30). Paul's method here is that of the allegorical exposition of
historical facts. He may have used the method to refute the
Judaizers by their own weapon, namely, their subtle, but puerile
presentations unauthorized by the Spirit. Paul meets this with

no fanciful imaginings of his own, but with an allegorical interpretation inspired by the Spirit of God. Just as the extraordinarily born Isaac, the gift of grace according to promise, supplanted the naturally-born Ishmael, so the new theocratic race, the spiritual seed of the promise — Gentile and Jewish believers together, has taken the place of those of the natural seed, who fondly assume themselves to belong to the kingdom by right of human birth and merit.

v. 21   Tell me, you who desire to be under law, do you not hear the law?

The term 'law' in the first part of the question is without the article, so that the reference is to general legal observances. In the second part, the allusion is to 'the law', to the Mosaic law book, the Pentateuch. Paul cuts in with this further consideration abruptly, as if excited by some new thought on the subject. The Galatians would become subject to law as an aid to their justification; but have they really paid attention to what the Book of the Law itself has to say? Some have supposed that the apostle is alluding to the actual listening to the law as constantly read in their hearing. They hear the words of Moses, but do not perceive their mystic sense. Paul's meaning is, however, more prosaic and precise than that. They desire to be under law, but they still do not listen to its plain and explicit teaching. When rightly understood, the law does not send us away from Christ; it sends us to Him and keeps us with Him. The law shows who are the true children of the promise; not those who are in bondage to it, but those who are freed men by grace and thus free men in Christ. By an act of their own self-will, the Galatians have developed a dread 'desire' for legal niceties and necessities (cf. v. 9), but they did not 'take to heart', for all that, what is the whole drift and destination of the law's teaching. They pick and choose. And where law is concerned that just cannot be done.

v. 22   For it is written that Abraham had two sons, one by a slave and one by a free woman.

The reference here is not to a specific passage, but serves rather as an introduction to the general account given in Genesis 16; 17; and 21. The bondwoman is, of course, Hagar; the free woman, Sarah. Hagar was an Eygptian slave in Abraham's house. The law and the promise come under the one roof. Nonetheless the law has a foreign origin and a slave position.

v. 23   But the son of the slave was born according to the flesh, the son of the free woman through promise.

Hagar's son, Ishmael, was Abraham's son by natural generation, while the son of the free woman, Isaac, was a gift of grace according to the promise. The 'But' which opens the sentence brings to the fore a strong contrast between the law and the promise. What one is, the other excludes. Paul is taking the plain facts of the historic account of the coming upon the stage of history of the slave-born offspring of Hagar and of the free-born offspring of Sarah. The former was a product of the common course of nature; the latter was the result of a divine promise. Two realms are thus set in antithesis; that of the present visible sphere of human existence, the flesh, and that of the invisible spiritual realm of grace and faith enshrined in the promise.

v. 24   Now this is an allegory:

Paul indicates that the Old Testament record itself is not a mere allegorical tale. His meaning is that these things are said allegorically since the story itself has another meaning besides the historical one. Yet by an allegory, Paul does not intend a mere illustration. He sees a spiritual truth embodied in the history, 'a shadow from the eternal world cast upon the sands of time'. In this particular account of Hagar and Sarah, Paul seems to be taking up a well-known mode of exegesis. At the same time, in a Christian context, much of the vagueness and vagaries of the rabbinical school were shed, and an authority other than that of Jewish rabbis was the source of that allegory which the apostolic writers sometimes used (cf. Jn. 16. 12–15; Eph. 3.5 etc.).

these women are two covenants.

The two women represent two covenants; Hagar's child was born 'under bondage' and thus is likened to the covenant of law which can only bear children unto bondage. The freewoman, too, as previously stated by the apostle (cf. 3. 15, 16), is the subject of 'the promise', and is thus an allegory of what is elsewhere characterized as a 'new' (Mt. 26. 28), or 'better' covenant (Heb. 8. 6) (cf. Jer. 31. 31).

One is from Mount Sinai, bearing children for slavery; she is Hagar.

Promulgated from Mount Sinai, the covenant of which Hagar is the type can only bring forth children after her kind. As a slave woman her offspring must share her status. Those who put themselves in Hagar's camp come under Sinai's covenant and find themselves in the position of slaves in bondage to the law (cf. 4. 1). Paul's concern is with the results of the covenant of law. He would make clear to the Galatians the condition into which submission to legal requirements must inevitably land them.

v. 25   Now Hagar is Mount Sinai in Arabia;

Both the construction and meaning here are uncertain. Paul does, however, indicate some connection between Hagar and Mount Sinai. Chrysostom refers to the work by the traveller, Havant, who says that the Arabians called Sinai, Hagar, by which they meant a 'rock' or 'stone'. Little credit has been given, however, to this remark by recent commentators. Hagar certainly fled to Arabia twice (cf. Gen. 16. 21), and the mount and city took their name from her, and the people were called Hagarites or Hagarenes. Thus, perhaps, is Sinai, with its rugged rock and outside the promised land, made to represent the law which inspired horror and brought into that bondage of which Hagar is the type, Paul, of course, was familar with Arabia (cf. 1. 17), and the association of Hagar with the place could have been known to the Galatians. The Galatians were seeking by their hankering after legalism to give to Hagar, as an allegory of the covenant of works, the status of authenticity and acceptability. But for Paul that can never be. Hagar was not the true wife of Abraham, nor is Sinai the true way of justification. Hagar brought forth children to slavery, so Sinai produces conditions of bondage. Some scholars would omit the reference to Hagar altogether from the text here and would regard Arabia, the country of Ishmael's descendants, as representing the off-spring of the bondwoman. But the reasons for the omission are far from conclusive. The retention of Hagar seems to accord best with the allegorical method of interpretation which the whole passage illustrates.

she corresponds to the present Jerusalem,

This Hagar, representative of Mount Sinai in Arabia, 'corresponds to', literally 'stand in the same row', as the Jerusalem which now is. Paul is here linking Judaism with the present Jerusalem of which it was the centre. Jerusalem was for Judaism, and for the Judaizers, the sacred home of the whole apparatus of legalistic religion, and the pomp and circumstances of the cultus. It was the veritable 'Vatican' of Judaism: and its teachers who had come to Galatia, were bent on binding the believers there to its system and its requirements.

for she is in slavery with her children.

The covenant of Sinai is represented by Hagar and belongs to the same set as the Jerusalem which now is. The condition of bondage into which the provisions and prohibitions of the Sinaitic covenant brought the people of the past is the same as that which marks the present Jerusalem. The Jerusalem which now is, is the home of the religion of bondage, which shuts up God in a temple made with hands and substitutes for His spiritual worship a scrupulous observance of legal enactments.

v. 26   But the Jerusalem above is free,

Unexpectedly, the contrast with the Jerusalem which now is, is not the Jerusalem which shall be, but the Jerusalem which is above. The true antithesis is between two types of religion; one having its source 'from below', and the other 'from above' (cf. Heb. 12. 22; Rev. 21. 2; see Col. 3. 1, 2; Phil. 3. 20). Bondage is the mark of legal religion; freedom characterizes the gospel of grace in Christ. The phrase 'is free' links up with the declaration made concerning Sarah in verses 22, 23. From this heavenly Jerusalem come the children of the free woman; here is the home of free worship of God in the Spirit — of sons serving in love, and not of slaves working in fear.

and she is our mother.

The 'our' is emphatic: the Jerusalem which is above, like Sarah, is free. In grace we are brought into a free society. This faith-freedom assures family-freedom. The background of the expression is the allegory of Hagar and Sarah, who brought forth children after their own status. The Jerusalem which is above, 'being as she is' is free and bears children unto freedom; as such she is the mother of the free.

v. 27   For it is written,

> 'Rejoice, O barren one that dost not bear;
> break forth and shout, thou who art not in travail;
> for the desolate hath more children
> than she who hath a husband.'

The quotation comes from the Septuagint version of Isaiah 54. 1. The prophecy is a song of triumph anticipating the deliverance of God's afflicted ones. God had deserted Israel and she mourns her widowhood; but she is to be restored and become the mother of a great and prosperous people. The image of conjugal union to represent the relation between God and His people is drawn out in verses 5 and 6 of the chapter in Isaiah. In chapter 51. 2, God's dealings with Abraham and Sarah point to His dealings with their descendants. Jewish writers have consistently connected the two passages. The apostle uses the quotation to bring out the idea that the glory of the Jerusalem which is from above, eclipses far that of the Jerusalem that now is. The prophet himself suggests such an application of his words, beyond their more immediate reference to the return of the exiles to repeople the city which had been made barren and waste, by the way he represents God as Redeemer not of Israel only, but of the whole earth (cf. v. 5), who will act for the people 'with great mercies' and 'with everlasting kindness' (vv. 6, 7). The barren can be taken to refer to Sarah as a type of the new dispensation; while she who hath a husband is Hagar. But it was Sarah, as the barren woman, who brought forth the child of the promise. So, likewise, has that Jerusalem which is from above become the rejoicing mother of a redeemed multitude, Jews and Gentiles, born to be free.

v. 28   Now we, brethren, like Isaac, are children of promise.

Once again the apostle appeals to his readers, by taking up Isaac to reinforce the point of the allegory (cf. v. 23). It is, however, uncertain whether the text should read 'we' or 'you', 'brethren'. The 'you' would thrust more directly upon the Galatians the fact that they are true sons of the free woman. Their standing before God does not depend upon any physical action but on God's own promise. They are children of the spiritual Jerusalem begotten through the gospel unto the adoption of sons. They are 'children of the promise' (Rom. 9. 8).

v. 29   But as at that time he who was born according to the flesh persecuted him who was born according to the Spirit, so it is now.

The contrast in this verse marks a difference between agency and attitude, characteristic of those after the flesh and those after the Spirit. He who was born according to the flesh of Abraham was, of course, Ishmael. But Paul daringly, it would seem, suggests that Isaac's birth was according to the Spirit. And in a profound sense it was, so that Paul is perfectly justified in his suggestion. Isaac's birth was in some sense a special act of God since both parents were well beyond the years of producing children. In this way, Paul can use it as an allegory of our spiritual birth by the Spirit of God. The agency, in the case of Ishmael, was the natural course of human birth; while in Isaac's case it wore the aspect of a special divine intervention.

THE BLESSINGS OF FAITH

Right from the beginning, there was tension between Hagar and Sarah. Hagar 'mocked' Sarah (cf. Gen. 21. 9, 10). Paul, recalling that the Hagarites became the historic enemies of Israel (cf. I Chron. 5. 10, 19; Ps. 86. 6), intensifies the word by rendering it 'persecuted', although this accords well with the circumstances of the story in Genesis 21. 9f. By giving the term this added connotation of active hostility the apostle is the better able to use the ancient account allegorically. Paul thus sees, at least indirectly, in the treatment of Gen. 21. 9 the relationship between the two brothers which developed between their progeny. Hagar's feelings towards her mistress were continued in her son; and the same attitude of spiteful opposition and of hateful antipathy was taken up by him who was born according to the flesh to him who was born according to promise. And so it ever is: true believers will ever be the occasion for the unbelievers' sting and scorn; and the persecution will come more cruelly and consistently from those, who, out of a false view of God, suppose that they will merit His favour by works of their own and by forcing others to do likewise. But always will Hagar and Sarah; Ishmael and Isaac; those of the Jerusalem which now is and those of the Jerusalem which is above; those born according to the flesh and those born according to the Spirit, be at odds; always will there be hostility between the two brothers; him of the slave woman and him of the free woman.

v. 30 *But what does the scripture say? "Cast out the slave and her son; for the son of the slave shall not inherit with the son of the free woman."*

The quotation is from Gen. 21. 10, but Paul changes the wording at the end of the verse while keeping the sense. Instead of 'for my son Isaac' he has 'the son of the free woman'. Against the treatment meted out by him who was born according to the flesh to him born of the Spirit, the apostle now enters a 'But' of counterblast and comfort. With the expulsion of Hagar went out the slave-born son. The son of the bondwoman had no place of inheritance with the son of the free. Hagar and Ishmael were driven forth beyond the pale of God's special guardianship and grace, away, as it were, from his covenant of promise. And so the apostle traces out the allegorical meaning of the story in order to make clear the fact that the two systems are forever irreconcilable, law and promise, salvation by works and salvation by grace. Paul has not, perhaps, in mind here the rejection of Israel as a nation, as he has in Romans 11. He is considering rather an attitude of mind and a habit of heart, namely, that of slavish adherence to legal necessities on the one hand, and of acceptance by faith of God's offer of salvation on the other.

It is the antithesis between salvation as a goal to be achieved and salvation as a gift to be received. Those who seek it in the former way shall never find it, 'for the son of the slave shall not inherit with the son the free woman'. So Paul is telling the Galatians, once again, in his allegorical use of the Hagar story, that it is a grave and perilous course on which they are being urged to embark, to forsake the way of sonship and freedom for that of slavery and bondage. Sarah's is the way to safety; Hagar's is the way to hopelessness. And there is no mean and no meeting-place between the two.

v. 31   So, brethren, we are not children of the slave but of the free woman.

This is a fitting finale to his exposition; a challenging conclusion. The Greek omits the article before 'slave', and by so doing gives the term a qualitative emphasis. We are not children of *any* slave; not in bondage to *any* system; rather we are children of *the* free woman, of the one and only spiritual kingdom, the Jerusalem which is above. This verse comes as a final inference from Paul's allegorical lessons. It comes with an opening, 'so then' (Phillips). Paul, including himself with the Galatians in the 'we' of the text, and, of course, with him all who belong to the household of faith, makes his grand declaration of independence by declaring that we are not children of a slave and therefore having that status, but of the free woman and therefore free. Throughout the section he has been specifying certain allegorical antitheses although he does not draw these out sharply. Despite this these may be set out side by side somewhat as follows:

The bondwoman and her son	The free woman and her son
Birth after the natural order 'after the flesh'	Birth out of the spiritual order 'after the Spirit'
Ishmael — the slave 'bondage'	Isaac — the son 'freedom'
Hagar driven to the desert with her son	Sarah abides in the house with her son
The Old Covenant Law	The New Covenant Promise
The earthly Jerusalem	The heavenly Jerusalem
Natural birth unto bondage	Spiritual birth unto freedom
Persecuting	Persecuted
Expulsion	Inheritance

A Practical Section — Ethical

In which Paul Justifies his Morals

5. 1—6. 10

This section is designed to show that the doctrine of justification by faith through union with Christ, far from loosening the bonds of morality, as the Judaizers alleged, rather presents and establishes a loftier, and at the same time, a really attainable ethical ideal. It is because men are free in Christ that they can be exhorted. Slaves can be commanded; free men are commended. Christian freedom, the apostle has already made clear, is based upon redemption. In this state and status men are truly free; but they must not relapse into slavery. In his doctrinal section, Paul has asserted that any measure of a return to legalism makes the assumption that justification and life depend upon the performance of certain requirements of law. Such a notion, he has steadily and successfully repudiated. Now, however, in this practical section, he makes the point that freedom does not mean excess; for freedom involves responsibilities. It is never for the Christian to say, 'I can do what I like'. It is always for the Christian to say, 'I will do what Christ likes'. The whole section deals with practical morality in wide sweep, in which the apostle discusses the aspects and the activities of the Christian life.

9

ASPECTS OF THE CHRISTIAN LIFE

5. 1–26

(i) Stand fast in the liberty of Christ 1–12

v. 1   For freedom Christ has set us free;

Taking the rendering of the text as it stands in our translation, the declaration has the force of an independent sentence. (The 'therefore' of the AV is based on inferior MSS. evidence.) The words are not, then, to be linked with the preceding verse (4. 31), but they form a sort of summary of the whole argument of the doctrinal section. We have been liberated in Christ that we might be free, and not that we should be slaves. We have been set free for freedom, and not set free to be brought again under a yoke of bondage. It is against the background of Christ's redemptive work that Paul sets this pregnant statement, partly by way of conclusive inference, and partly by way of challenging irony. The word need hardly be said; it is so obvious and yet it had to be said, succinctly, stabbingly and surely.

stand fast therefore, and do not submit again to a yoke of slavery.

In freedom we are to make a firm stand. The call is to stand fast in freedom. The Galatians were slipping out of it; that was the tragedy of their posture. They were on the slopes not on the firm ground. It is only as they stand fast in freedom can they really stand firm in faith. The recurrence of the 'again' is, then, significant. They have been brought out of the slavery of heathenism, and they may not be going to return to that, but they seem ready to submit to the bondage of Judaism (cf. 4. 9).

The word to them is, therefore, not to 'bow their necks' to a yoke of bondage; and there is no article before 'yoke', for any system of slavery must be inappropriate, and should be unacceptable to those who for freedom have been set free in Christ. So the call to them is to take a firm stand, and 'Be not careless, but steadfast and constant. Lie not down and sleep, but stand up' (Luther). For to stand fast in liberty is not to be stuck fast through laziness.

v. 2   Now I, Paul, say to you that if you receive circumcision, Christ will be of no advantage to you.

Paul now, emphatically, asserts his apostolic authority which he has vindicated, and repudiates the notion that circumcision has any value, and that he had preached it as such (cf. v. 11). For the first time in the letter the question of circumcision, the issue which lay behind the whole controversy as it relates to the Gentiles, is brought out into the open (cf. 2. 3–8, 12). If the Galatians receive circumcision, or if they allow themselves to be circumcised with the idea that it is somehow necessary for justification, then, declares the apostle, 'Christ will be of no use to you at all' (Phillips). Quite evidently this was the rite that the Judaizers were seeking to impose upon the Galatians; yet Paul is possibly using the term not just for this particular ritual, but as a symbol for Judaistic legalism in general. There is a terrible and telling logic in Paul's declaration that by undergoing circumcision Christ shall be of no advantage to them. For he who has himself circumcised really disbelieves in the power of grace and the adequacy of Christ. As Chrysostom says, 'He who disbelieves can profit nothing by that grace which he disbelieves'. The future tense, 'shall profit nothing', does not refer so much to a time in the future, as to the certainty of the result which must follow from wanting circumcision. Far from being the seal of a sonship in Christ, circumcision would be for them no less than the sacrament of the excision from Christ. It is by reliance upon Christ's work alone that salvation is secured. By distrust in it, salvation is brought to peril; while by disbelieving in it, salvation is forfeited.

v. 3 I testify again to every man who receives circumcision that he is bound to keep the whole law.

This verse reiterates with added solemnity the thought of the previous one. Paul would 'again' bear witness to the truth of the gospel. He has done so many times before; certainly when he first came to Galatia, and before the other apostles in Jerusalem and Antioch. This letter is yet another witness against those who would make Christ's word of no effect. In the presence, as it were, of God as his witness (cf. Eph. 4. 17), Paul sets down a further consideration why the rite cannot be made binding. Not only do those who want themselves circumcised lose the advantage which relationship to Christ by faith brings, but they take upon themselves an added burden too heavy to be borne. No one can carry out the obligations of circumcision without undertaking the whole round of legal prescriptions. Once the validity of legalism is admitted in one particular, then the validity of its every demand must be allowed. But who is sufficient to follow out in full detail all that the law requires?

v. 4 You are severed from Christ, you who would be justified by the law;

While the apostle is restating verse 2, he does so here in a direct address — 'you'; you who would be justified by the law are 'brought to nought' as regards grace. The expression is a forceful one showing that the acceptance of legalism spells out the abandonment of Christ. There can be no common ground between the two ways; they stand opposed. To be severed from Christ is to become void from Him so as to make His work of no effect (cf. 3. 17). The connection with Christ is no longer operative; and those who pursue the legal way have set themselves outside the sphere where God can receive them. This is the state of the outcast. The present tense of design brought out in the phrase, 'you who would be justified', is intended to make clear the hopelessness of the endeavour. Those who seek to bring about their standing before God as righteous in His sight by way of law, are destined to be rejected, because they have cut themselves off from Him in whom alone they have their acceptance at the throne of the most High.

123

you have fallen away from grace.

Grace denotes the condition of man's acceptance with God, and to fall away from grace is to step out of the grace-way. The issue here is not whether a believer can fall from a state of grace and be lost. Paul is concerned with the subject of justification. He is making the point that to take to the law-way is to abandon the grace-way. No one can walk the two roads at once; indeed they are distant from each other, and run in opposite directions. No one can live the life of faith in Christ as the sole ground of filial relationship with the God of grace, and, at the same time, live the live of slavish obedience to the requirements demanded by legalism. There are no two ways about it: to give in to the works-way is to fall from the grace-way. The former leads to banishment with Hagar, the mother of legalism; the latter brings into blessing with Sarah, the mother of promise. Cutting loose from grace is to become cut off from Christ.

v. 5 For through the Spirit, by faith, we wait for the hope of righteousness.

This verse brings out into contrast the 'fallen' state of the previous verse and the 'faith' state of this one. The 'For' introduces an argument from the opposite (cf. 3. 10); 'for we', on the other side, who are Christ's, wait in hope. *You* turn to the flesh: *we* live in the Spirit. *You* set yourselves to keep the law: *we* take the way of faith. To abide in Christ is to continue in grace: to abandon Christ is to become cut off from grace. Through the Spirit, the believer waits for the hope of righteousness. This does not mean that righteousness is in doubt — that the believer lives with a vague hope. The Judaizers 'hoped' to satisfy God's demands. But those who are under grace wait the fulfilment of their hope. It is certain, as it is the whole purpose of the epistle to maintain, that the believer is already 'accepted as righteous', fully and freely, here and now. What is hoped for with confidence is the future consummation in righteousness, when the righteousness in which we are now accepted will, by God's progressive inworking, be finally and perfectly realized. The 'hope' is not, the sentiment, but the concrete reality; the thing hoped for. And for that we wait, as it were, with eager expectation. And wait we must; for the realization of our justification in righteousness, no more than God's acceptance of us as righteous, is of works. We wait in faith, but we work in fear. The hope for which we wait is the positive certainty of the verdict of final acquittal which has already been assured in our justification.

v. 6   For in Christ Jesus neither circumcision nor uncircumcision is of any avail,

This verse removes every lingering doubt that some ritual act or legal action could be admitted as an aid to justification. Whether or not one is circumcised does not matter. Neither the one state nor the other has any value for salvation. All that matters is being 'in Christ'. Abraham was circumcised after he was justified by faith; Paul was circumcised before, but neither the absence of the rite nor its presence was of any saving significance (cf. 6. 15; 1 Cor. 7. 19). What Paul then declares, without equivocation, is that from the Christian standpoint nothing avails but union with Christ. This is the one all-determining factor; the only marking fact.

but faith working through love.

When Paul speaks of faith, he is uncovering the very essence of Christianity subjectively, as Christ, for him, specified the very heart of it objectively. But by adding the phrase 'working through love', the apostle makes a significant stress. For the first time in this epistle the term 'love' appears; and for the only time in his letters are the two terms, 'faith' and 'love', brought together into immediate connection. Yet the association is important in the context of his general purpose in *Galatians*, and especially is it so in this section in which he is elucidating his ethical teaching. By faith, Paul means, of course, that personal commitment to Christ which results in the experience of the indwelling Christ as the motive and master power of the believer's moral life. It is in this context that the unexpected qualification, faith *working through love*, must be understood. Ruled out right away is the false view that Paul is here declaring love to be the believer's subjective ground of justification.

Faith, it is true, may be made to grow in us through love; but it is not, in the first instance, wrought in us by love. Such a notion would be itself a return to that very Galatianism from which the apostle would have us delivered.

Love is not, then, here joined with faith as the principle of justification, but as the principle of works which follow justification. The Judaizers upheld circumcision from the notion that the law was binding. By this statement, Paul implies that the law has been set aside by being fulfilled in the one word 'love' (cf. 5. 14). A faith working through love will not occasion strife (cf. 5. 15, 16). Any suggestion by the legalists that by doing away with law, Paul is really robbing life of its moral goal and goad, is thus countered by his emphasis upon the dynamic nature of faith which generates love as the ordered standard and the operative spring of Christian conduct. Some scholars prefer to take 'love' here to refer to God's love for us, rather than the believer's love for others. The verse is then read as a declaration that the supreme question is not whether or not one has been circumcised, but whether, in view of the revelation of His love, we have come to faith in Him. In this case, what makes a man right with God is his faith quickened into life by a sense of God's constraining love in Christ (cf. 2 Cor. 5. 14). No verse, perhaps, in the whole epistle so surely announces the spiritual nature of the Christian gospel. No ritual conditions and no physical requirements of any kind have any place in establishing man's acceptance with God. Love is then the fruit of justifying faith, as faith is the energy of authenticating love.

v. 7 You were running well; who hindered you from obeying the truth?

Paul now turns to the Galatians in a series of abrupt and unconnected statements, in which he remonstrates with them. The question of this verse is itself an appeal, arising out of the recollection of their former conduct and the awareness of their present compromise. You were running well, says the apostle, drawing a metaphor from the foot-races of the stadium. All seemed to have been going fine and the apostle was rejoicing in the knowledge. But then news came that the Galatians had faltered. Who can have 'put you off the course'? (Phillips), he asks rhetorically. By someone they had been checked in mid career. The term translated 'hindered' is a military one, and has the idea of being 'impeded' in one's progress by an enemy, who has managed to dig up the road or destroy the bridges, or by some other method seeks to hamper one's onward movement. The form of the question implies that whoever he was who introduced the obstacles, it was not one to whom they should have listened and looked. By 'the truth' Paul means the Gospel which comes not only as a Person to be trusted, but also as a message to be obeyed. By introducing the word 'obey', Paul is indicating, what he will later expound, that a faith working through love is not a faith acting in licence.

v. 8   This persuasion is not for him who called you.

That 'persuasion' of not obeying the truth to which the Galatians were being induced to yield, is not of Him, who called them. The One who called them is, of course, God. Elsewhere in the epistle, the apostle omits the name God; but here, as there, he leaves the reader clearly to supply the missing word (cf. 2. 8; 3. 5). The phrase rendered 'him who called you', is in the present tense; for He who has called, is still calling the Galatians in His never-failing grace into the grace that never fails. Some think that the use of the present tense puts the emphasis upon the *person* who does the calling rather than on the *act* of calling itself.

v. 9   A little leaven leavens the whole lump.

The Galatians should have known that by the teachings of Christ (cf. Mt. 16. 12; see 13. 23), and from their own present experience, how speedily does a little error permeate the whole area of truth. The words come again in 1 Cor. 5. 6 and seem to have become a well-known proverb. Here Paul uses it to reveal the danger to the Galatians of mixing the gospel with a little legalism. Only too soon would its purity become corrupted. The leaven can either refer to the 'persuasion' of the previous verse, or to the influence of some bad individual (cf. v. 7).

v. 10   I have confidence in the Lord that you will take no other view than mine;

The apostle now comforts himself with the thought that the Galatians will return to the truth of the gospel. The 'I' and 'you' are emphatic. However much others might lose confidence in them, Paul would not be one of them. He knows them and has happy memories of their past standing and zeal. The apostle's confidence is not, however, born just out of a happy situation; it is a confidence cradled in the Lord. Here is both the sphere of his assurance and the bond of his union with the Galatian believers (cf. 2 Thess. 3. 4). His confidence is that they 'will not take any fatal step' (Phillips), or 'the wrong view' (NEB). Paul would have them think, as he does, on the great subject of justification; for any other view would be bound to lead them along the wrong track. He, therefore, either bids them to follow his course, for though no direct command immediately preceded the words the fact may be implied, or he appeals to them to be as they were before the coming of the corrupter into their midst.

and he who is troubling you will bear his judgement, whoever he is.

Whoever he is who is worrying and unsettling them, even if he cannot be identified openly, shall carry an oppressive burden. Upon him shall the judgement of God fall; and it will be a punishment consonant with the evil intent of seeking to lay upon God's people a weight which God Himself has not required them to carry. The phrase 'whoever he is' shows how seriously the apostle takes the situation which is developing in Galatia as a result of the presence there of false teaching. Be the one responsible ever so highly regarded, he will not escape the divine judgement (cf. 1. 7–9).

v. 11   But if I, brethren, still preach circumcision, why am I still persecuted?

There is no clear break between this verse and what has just been said. Evidently, however, at this point the malicious rumour of his opponents comes back to the apostle's mind. Paul has condemned circumcision as unnecessary and useless;

but his enemies, possibly with the case of Timothy in mind, asserted that he still admitted circumcision. What then is the position? This: Paul did allow the rite in the case of the Jews (cf. Acts 16. 1f.). He would not have the Jew wilfully isolate himself and give unnecessary offence. In so far as the Christian profession was not compromised, it was all to the good. Circumcision was a national affair, and Paul did not ask the Jew to denationalize himself. As a national bond it could stand for the Jew. But it had no value as a precondition for salvation for the Jew, and no application at all to the Gentile.

The apostle answers the charge made against him regarding circumcision by asking the pointed question, Why is he still suffering persecution if so be he is still advocating circumcision? He makes, therefore, a direct appeal to the actual facts of the situation. His point is simply; 'Why if I still Judaize, do the Judaizers still persecute me?' It is his opponents who are inconsistent. They begin by persecuting the apostle for not demanding that the Gentiles should be circumcised, and now they say that he still recognises it and sometimes requires it. They cannot have it both ways. There is a touch of irony in Paul's retort; if they do really believe that I continue to preach circumcision, then why do they persecute me for not doing so!

In that case the stumbling block of the cross has been removed.

This statement may be taken either as ironical or logical. If in the first way, then Paul is saying that if indeed he does preach circumcision then the cross, the occasion of offence, has dropped out of his preaching, so there is no reason why he should suffer persecution. If the words are to be interpreted in the second way, then Paul is pressing home to the Galatians the logic of his position. Should it be maintained that by preaching circumcision as necessary, then the reiterated objection that his doctrine of the cross makes circumcision unnecessary has no point. It was the cross, above all else in apostolic teaching, which was the scandal (cf. 1 Cor. 1. 23). Paul could well recall here his own pre-conversion attitude to the cross. It had once been for him the focus of his persecuting zeal; now it was for him the centre of his preaching power. Once he had regarded the cross with high-handed aversion; now he approaches the cross with humble-souled adoration. The cross, of course, did not mean for Paul the rugged wood or the mere symbol; the cross was for him the efficacy of the atoning death of Christ.

v. 12   I wish those who unsettle you would mutilate themselves!

As Paul thinks of the situation, he breaks out in righteous indignation against those who would throw the Galatians off balance. He wishes that those who would cut off the Galatians from their true home in the faith of the gospel would cut themselves off from the household of faith. Why, Paul wonders, do these Judaizers stop short at circumcision; with the pleasure they take in mere physical acts, why do they not go on to mutilate themselves like the heathen priests of Cybele? That would be the logic of their position; and that would cut them off indeed from the congregation of those justified by faith through union with Christ. If only they who would cut your bodies would cut themselves so as to cut themselves off — then would the situation be easier for the Galatians, and the way of renewal assured.

(ii)   Walk on in the liberty of Christ

Stressing that liberty works in the sphere of love, Paul enters a polemic against the antinomian abuse of the doctrine. Freedom is not to be equated with self-indulgence.

(a)   Liberty works in Love

v. 13   For you were called to freedom, brethren;

The 'you' is emphatic and suggests a contrast between 'you', the Galatians, who know the truth, as opposed to those who were troubling them. The declaration is again a summary statement of the whole preceding exposition (cf. v. 1a). By translating the Greek phrase as 'for' the point is made that it is, 'for' 'freedom' — for the free way of faith, that we have been called. Verse one of this chapter can be regarded as a summary of the apostle's warnings against the Judaizers: this passage is a summary statement of the freedom enjoyed by those who are 'in

Christ'. But Paul takes immediate opportunity to guard the doctrine against antinomian perversions of it.

only do not use your freedom as an opportunity for the flesh,

Here is the preventing and preserving clause introduced by his use of the term 'only' (cf. 1. 23; 2. 10). The word 'only' is for his readers a sort of hinge by which the apostle's thought turns from his bold assertion of Christian freedom to the contrasting danger of abusing it. Liberty must not become an occasion for the flesh to take hold. It must not be allowed to become its basis of operation, Paul declares by the use of his own special word rendered 'opportunity' (cf. Rom. 7. 8, 11; 2 Cor. 5. 12; 11. 12; 1 Tim. 5. 14). The term 'flesh', in contrast with the physical reference earlier in the epistle, has, in this and the following sections, an ethical meaning expressing the condition of human nature under the domain of evil. Our lower nature is not to be made the starting-point from which sin can extend its mastery. The flesh is not to be allowed to become a spring-board for folly.

but through love be servants of one another.

This is the apostle's answer to the legalism of the Judaizers and to the license of the antinomians. There is an article before the term 'love'. Through *the* love; love is, perhaps, personified. Through Him who is The Love we can alone serve. It implies, therefore, the idea of servitude; and is used here purposely because of the emphatic assertion of freedom which immediately precedes. Paul has been arguing that the Galatians are not to be led into bondage; now he asserts that the only bondage is love. Free as to legalism we are bound as to love. To act in love as slaves for our fellows is to be really free. The Christian's prayer to God must then ever be; 'O Lord, "Make slaves the partners of Thy throne" '; and the Christian's practice in godliness must always be that of slavery in love of others for Jesus' sake.

v. 14   For the whole law is fulfilled in one word, 'You shall love your neighbour as yourself.'

For the Judaizers and their sympathizers this must have come as a startlingly new truth, although the Old Testament had announced it, and the Christ of the New Testament had restated it. But the words are a paradox. For Paul has been contending with all persuasiveness and passion that for salvation man is under no obligation to keep any of the law's requirements; now he declares that they will fulfill all the law who live in love's servitude one for another. But the paradox is not without sense and significance. For by his use of the term law in this passage the apostle is not intending that love to one's neighbour is measured by legalistically fulfilling the law. Rather is he concerned here with the law as an ethical principle of the divine purpose which a man obeys in love through the Spirit. In this one requirement the 'whole law' is completed and performed. The idea of the law's totality is strongly expressed by the position of the article — the whole law.

The term 'neighbour' of Lev. 19. 18 refers to the Jewish people. It was our Lord who enlarged its scope to bring in others also (cf. Lk. 10. 29f.). The message summarily stated in this verse is expanded by Paul in Rom. 13. 8–10, where the apostle tells us that the only real debt we owe any man is that of love. The entire law is fulfilled, and filled full, in this one word: You shall love your neighbour as yourself. As self-love is a necessity for one's own well-being, a like love of one's neighbour, made possible in the love of God, makes for the well-being of others. With an eye, therefore, on the ethical demands of social relationships, the apostle enforces Christ's law of love.

v. 15 But if you bite and devour one another take heed that you are not consumed by one another.

If, instead of loving one another as Christians should, we 'go on fighting one another, tooth and nail' (NEB) as Christians shouldn't, the result will not be mutual helpfulness but mutual destruction. The words are put hypothetically, but the Galatians were in reality doing these things. Their legalism quenched their love. And without love everything is amiss. To lose love is to become like salt that has lost its saltness; it is to become useless beyond the hope of recovery.

(b) Liberty is found in Obedience to the Spirit

Paul has made the point that liberty works within the sphere of love. Now under the same general heading of going on in the liberty of Christ, he makes clear that liberty is found in subjection to the Spirit. The terms 'flesh' and 'Spirit' are brought into contrast; into conflict indeed; as also is the relation between 'law' and 'Spirit'. Flesh and law are closely allied; both move within the same sphere, the outward and the material. Far from the law being a safe-guard against the flesh, as the Judaizers fondly supposed, it acts rather as a stimulus. To renounce the flesh is to renounce the law, and that means to lead the life of the Spirit. Here, then, Paul announces the germ ideas which he works out in fuller exposition in Romans (cf. ch. 8).

v. 16   But I say, walk by the Spirit, and do not gratify the desires of the flesh.

But this, I say, or more specifically, 'This is what I mean'. Paul is referring back to verse 13. The call to walk is a frequent injunction in Paul's writings (cf. Rom. 6. 4; 8. 1; 13. 13; 14. 15; 1 Cor. 3. 3; 7. 17; 2 Cor. 4. 2; 5. 7; 10. 2, 3; 12. 18; Eph. 2. 2, 10 etc.). It is virtually a synonym for 'to live', 'to conduct one's self'. And this walking is 'by the Spirit' as the rule and the power by which our behaviour is to be regulated. The preposition suggested by Paul's use of the dative could, with equal cogency, be made to read 'in the Spirit' (Phillips). In this case, the Spirit is regarded as the sphere within which and the path along which the life of freedom is to be lived out. The emphatic note is 'the Spirit'. They who conduct their lives in and whose lives are conducted by the Spirit, shall in no wise fulfil — a double negative with an emphatic future — the passions of the flesh. Paul is, of course, writing to those who have received the Spirit. When He is followed, then Christian liberty will not degenerate into licence. If the spirit that is within us is at ease under sin, then it is not a spirit which comes from the Holy Spirit by whom we are led (v. 18) and in whom we live (v. 25).

v. 17   For the desires of the flesh are against the Spirit, and the desires of the Spirit are against the flesh; for these are opposed to each other, to prevent you from doing what you would.

The reason why walking by the Spirit will exclude fulfilling the desires of the flesh is here given: the two are mutually exclusive and continuously opposed. The flesh, as human nature conditioned by evil, 'fights against' the Spirit; and the Spirit against the flesh. Between the two there is not, and never can be any alliance or cessation of hostilities. Flesh and Spirit are 'antagonistic' to each other. The aim of the contestants is to hinder the contrary willed action which is prompted by the one and the other. Yet the verse must not be interpreted to leave the impression of an indecisive conflict within the soul. The context suggests something full and final. Paul's words are a confident declaration that, though the flesh asserts itself against the Spirit, nevertheless the Spirit's desires are opposed to it. The clause 'to prevent you doing what you would' is added, not as applying to both statements equally, but with particular reference to the restraining action of the Spirit on the constraining attitudes of the flesh. The Spirit is set in opposition to the flesh so as to secure the result that we are no longer free to do what we please. In the life of the justified person there persists a conflict brought about by the presence of the Spirit whose desires are opposed to those of the natural man. Yet it is by the Spirit's very indwelling that we lose our freedom to do just what the flesh prompts and prefers.

v. 18   But if you are led by the Spirit you are not under the law.

The apostle now refers back to the idea of law, thereby associating it with flesh as operating within the same sphere of the outward and the material. He has declared that by walking in the Spirit we are free from submission to the law. The sudden introduction of the term 'law' here, as in verse 14, is a reminder that although Paul has come to the practical section of his epistle, the old issue is still the dominating one. The Galatians had been told by the Judaizers that as God demanded moral conduct from His worshippers the only safeguard against the deeds of the flesh was to order their lives according to the demands of law. The apostle shows that he is no less insistent upon right conduct, but, he asserts, those who order their lives along the Spirit's path and according to the Spirit's power have alone the prescription against the passions of the flesh. For such, the law no longer is a rigid rule and a taunting tyrant. Theirs will be the Law of the Spirit of Life in Christ Jesus by which they are free from the Law of Sin and Death.

(iii) Bear Fruit in the liberty of the Spirit

In these verses Paul marks out the characteristics of the two kinds of life; life in the flesh (vv. 19–21), and life in the Spirit (vv. 22–23). The fact of the believer's identity with Christ means that His death has a direct power upon him to nullify the flesh (vv. 24–25).

vv. 19–21a Now the works of the flesh are plain: immorality, impurity, licentiousness, idolatry, sorcery, enmity, strife, jealousy, anger, selfishness, dissension, party spirit, envy, drunkenness, carousing, and the like.

This is a challenging catalogue. How can it be ascertained that one is living one's whole life in the Spirit (cf. v. 16 Phillips), and is being led by Him? (v. 18) Plainly the test is the very practical one of the sort of life one is living. For 'the deeds of the flesh are quite obvious' (Moffatt). And they are 'works' of the flesh in contrast with the 'fruit' of the Spirit, because they are the outburst of the passions of the flesh. Some commentators have sought to put the sins mentioned into groups and to relate them to different types of persons. The first group of three arise directly from sensual passions; the second, 'idolatry' and 'sorcery', have to do with unlawful spiritual trafficking, prominent in the heathen religions. The next eight are all characterized by the element of hostility and hatred, and as such transgress openly the principle of brotherly love. The last two, 'drunkenness' and 'carousing', indicate that intemperate excess cannot be the mark of those who have life in the Spirit. But evidently the apostle did not intend his list to be a neat summary of all the evils to which the desires of the flesh can give vent, since he adds to his catalogue, 'and the like', or as we might say, et cetera.

There is no need to specify in any exact way the precise nature of the sin connoted by each word. To do so might be to let some out from under the umbrella. What Paul would have us understand is that all deeds such as these are works of human nature conditioned by the Fall. They are the deeds of the flesh upon which evil has taken hold to use as its basis of operation.

v. 21b   I warn you, as I warned you before, that those who do such things shall not inherit the kingdom of God.

On some previous occasion, possibly when he first preached the gospel to them as a necessary word for those emerging from heathenism, Paul had forewarned the Galatians concerning the deeds of the flesh. To persist in such acts would be evidence that they had not really experienced new life in the Spirit. The apostle, now once again, reinforces his warning. All who make a practice of these things can have 'no inheritance', as the phrase is literally, in the kingdom of God. The kingdom of God has here a future reference to the inauguration of the realm of God by Christ's return to reign in righteousness, when the kingdoms of this world become the kingdom of Christ and of God (Eph. 5. 5; cf. 1 Cor. 6. 9, 10; 15. 50; 2 Thess. 1. 5; 2 Tim. 4. 18).

vv. 22–23a   But the fruit of the Spirit is love, joy, peace, patience, kindness, goodness, faithfulness, gentleness, self-control;

The term 'fruit' is in the singular, for what the Spirit produces is a goodly 'harvest'. As 'fruit', they form, as it were, one cluster and as such are the natural expression in character of the divine life within (cf. Col. 3. 12–15). The 'fruit' of the Spirit ought to be distinguished from the 'gifts' of the Spirit of 1 Corinthians 12. 8–11. The gifts are particular powers bestowed sovereignly by the Spirit of God on men for special service. The fruit is a necessary product of the justified life; the very hallmark of its reality. The activities of the flesh, verses 19 to 21, are noisy, undisciplined, external: but the Spirit's action, by contrast, is quiet, controlled, inward. The term 'love', which heads the list of the Spirit's fruit, should not be regarded merely as one of the cluster; it is rather the stem upon which all the rest hangs. Love stands at the head of the list, but is the heart of the whole. In his catalogue of the virtues in Colossians, in which the apostle specifies the wardrobe of the redeemed life, he leaves love to the last item. Having listed the other garments, he adds, above all put on love as a golden girdle to bind all together into a settled harmony (cf. Col. 3. 14). According to Paul's thought in this passage, it is around love that the rest of the Spirit's fruit grows.

Paul is not, perhaps, giving us a specific classification of the ethical qualities which issue from the redeemed life. But 'joy' and 'peace' may be taken as love's attitude with regard to God. The Judaizers had a religion destitute of joy and drained of peace. But the true religion of the Spirit is characterized by both (cf. Rom. 14. 17; 15. 13). Patience, kindness, goodness, faithfulness are basic to love's attitude towards others. While gentleness and self-control are love's acceptance of restraint upon ourselves.

v. 23b against such there is no law.

The word 'such' suggests that Paul does not regard his list as a complete catalogue. These are but samples and signs of life in the Spirit. There is no law against such fruit as this. How could there be? For the purpose of the law is to restrain and to condemn; but where the Spirit reigns there can be no frustration and no condemnation. The law can only restrain, whereas the Spirit does but constrain (cf. 5. 18).

v. 24 And those who belong to Christ Jesus have crucified the flesh with its passions and desires.

Those who belong to Christ Jesus, or literally, 'they of Christ Jesus', are such as have 'put on Christ' (3. 27), and now live the Christ-life (2. 20). The phrase suggests a community. For those who are 'of Christ', constitute a redeemed family (cf. 4. 5), and are collectively Abraham's offspring and inheritors of the promise (cf. 3. 29).

The word for 'have crucified' is in the aorist tense, and may denote either a decisive change complete in itself, without reference to time, or it may have a direct historical reference, pointing back to the time when they came to belong to Christ. This last seems the most natural explanation. Thus the idea is that they had once and for all nailed to the cross, 'the flesh with its passions and deeds', when they became united to Him by their faith which they had sealed in baptism. In that state, the apostle would have them remain. The reference is not then to a process, but to an act done (cf. Rom. 6). Yet crucifixion was a lingering mode of death; so although the passions and deeds of the flesh are not yet robbed of their power, yet they can be left as crucified, and 'reckoned as dead'.

v. 25   If we live by the Spirit, let us also walk by the Spirit.

Although dead, the Christian is yet alive; but it is far from a living death that he lives. The unbeliever is living to die; the believer is dying to live! As in verse 18 this is a conditional clause supposing a present situation. Paul would, however, fain believe that the Galatians would not want anything other than to live by the Spirit. The causative dative, 'by the Spirit' or, better possibly, 'in the Spirit' means that if we are partakers of the new life of which the Spirit is the author, then we are to walk in the Spirit. The practice of the outward social life is to correspond to the principles of the inner spiritual life. The word 'walk' in this verse is not the same as that of verse 16. The literal meaning here is 'to walk in rank'. The reference is not, then, so much to individual conduct as to the life of a community under the Spirit's direction and dynamic.

v. 26   Let us have no self-conceit, no provoking of one another, no envy of one another

The community reference of this verse accords well with what he has just said. Living in the Spirit and walking therein is the sure preventative from vanity, rivalry, and jealousy. 'Let us not be', or 'become', or 'appear', any one of these. It may be that the spirit which these prohibitions indicate had not shown itself as yet; but the Galatians were becoming liable to it. And the conditions were such that it could easily develop. Self-conceit, or vanity, on its stronger side issues in 'provoking one another'; on its weaker side, it leads to envy. And none of these are of the Holy Spirit; all of them are of the flesh.

10

ACTIVITIES OF CHRISTIAN LIBERTY

6. 1–10

From a consideration of the aspects of Christian liberty, Paul turns to say something about its activites. He makes an appeal to the genuinely spiritual, in order to show how spiritual freedom issues in specific obligations.

(i) Christian freedom produces sympathy

v. 1   Brethren, if a man is overtaken in any trespass, you who are spiritual should restore him in a spirit of gentleness.

Paul opens the appeal with the word, 'Brothers' (cf. 1. 11; 5. 11; 6. 18), so as to express the fact of their unity with one another because of their union with Christ. A whole argument, therefore, lies hidden under this one designation. Paul would seem to have in mind a case of the most extreme nature as an illustration of what true brotherhood involves. A more exact translation of the phrase, should be 'even if' (Phillips); or, perhaps, it might be even better put, 'If a man even be overtaken in a fault'. The word for 'overtaken' holds in it the element of surprise. It is 'to be taken unawares', 'to be caught napping'. Such a one, 'you who are spiritual' are to take in hand.

There is no irony in the descriptive phrase; it means those who have indeed recognized the Spirit's sway in their lives; those who have paid full heed to the apostle's words. Such are alone qualified to act as restorers of those tripped up. And it is their duty to do so, and not to stand aloof. For to pass by on the other side, or to look down with fleeting pity, and then continue on their own way, would be to disprove their spirituality. As men, really and rightly under the Spirit, they will seek to set the fallen one back on the true path once again. The word for 'to restore' is connected with the mending of nets. A fallen brother has rent the fellowship and the rent must be mended. Some think that the word has a surgical origin and has to do with the setting of a bone or joint. Certainly, the one who has been caught out in a trespass has dislocated a bone in the body of the redeemed community and has put it 'out of joint'. It is the business of spiritual persons to undertake the task of resetting the bone; but 'very gently' (NEB), 'for a bone of Him shall not be broken' (cf. Jn. 19. 36; Eph. 5. 30). Nothing will be accomplished by denunciation. In 'a spirit of gentleness' will 'you who are spiritual' seek to put right an erring brother.

There is, perhaps, no better illustration of the dictum of the apostle's than this very letter itself. Throughout its pages, Paul does not utter violent vituperations; but rather shows surprise that the Galatians should reveal any tendency to fall out of line. All along, he believes the best and hopes to the end. Even his most passionate passages reveal him, not as the offended master but as the agonizing mother (cf. 4. 19).

Look to yourself, lest you too be tempted.

A necessary reminder to all; and even to the most mature. There is a transition from the plural to the singular, and the word 'look' is intensive. So the injunction is to look very carefully, each one to his own standing. It is all too easy to fall: high places are dizzy. The warning needs to be well taken by any who would help another back on the way. The temptation to become a Pharisee is very real. But love 'does not gloat over another man's sins' (1 Cor. 13. 6 NEB).

v. 2 Bear one another's burdens, and so fulfil the law of Christ.

The true test of discipleship is brotherliness, and this means mutual relationship. The legalists would impose 'burdens'. Here Paul says 'bear one another's burdens'; but it is love-burdens not law-burdens he is thinking of. If, however, it is still a law the Galatians want, then let it be 'the law of Christ', for that is the law of love (cf. 5. 14; see Mt. 22. 37–40). It is love that 'fills up to fulness' the law of Christ. The word for burden in this verse is different from that used in verse 5. This burden has the idea of a load shared by others, while in verse 5 it has the idea of a pack carried by each. The 'burden' is that of caring about, and suffering with, and responsibility for others, in their need, sin and guilt. But it also applies to any weight that spiritual men seek to lift that others may be helped on the way and encouraged along the path.

(ii) Christian freedom demands responsibility

v. 3   For if any one thinks he is something, when he is nothing, he deceives himself.

Such a one deceives himself by his own fancies, but he deceives nobody else. Such a 'somebody' is really a 'nobody'. The one who cannot admit to having any faults, will have little sympathy for one 'detected in some sin'. He is certainly not the sort of man who can make the failures of others his concern. His is but that vanity, which inflates his self-sufficiency, rather than that spirituality, which inspires his self-sacrifice. The best way to be something for others is to be everything for Christ (cf. 2. 20). It is the man who 'imagines' he is 'just it'; who palms off upon himself the illusion of his own spirituality and superiority, who is 'deluding himself'. Paul here has in mind the fancies of the would-be 'spiritual'. James, speaking of the man 'deceiving his own heart', has in mind the fictions of the would-be 'religious'. Both are really unbearable, just because they are not 'burden-bearers'. They are content in the remoteness of their self-lit heights; but they never lend a hand to help those caught out in the mire of the gloomy streets. They shed their responsibilities as they shroud themselves in their self-deception.

v. 4   But let each one test his own work,

Both terms, 'each' and 'his own', are emphatic. For the best check on pride is for each one to check his own work. Faith is to be tested by works. Here Paul links up with James (cf. Js 2. 18). The command, for so it is, should be read in connection with verses 2 and 3. The 'work' which a man may achieve by his own efforts, and which might be an occasion for self-congratulation, is the very work the value of which he must 'assess properly' (Phillips).

and then his reason to boast will be in himself alone and not in his neighbour.

Each individual man should put his work to the test to prove of what nature is his own conduct. And should there be the least ground for self-glorification it will then be in himself alone and not in unpleasant comparison with others (cf. Mt. 7. 1–5). The inflated egoist, who can but boast of his own high standing, in comparison with one who has fallen, does not perceive his own delusion or recognize his own danger. The truth is, however, that the only ground for glorying such a man has, is the position in which he thinks himself to be secure, and which he fancies is his when seen in the light of the shortcomings of others. It is the man who examines his own works who may have some reason for self-commendation; but even in his case it will be only 'in himself', and not in that other person; not in the man who is other than himself. And in the last reckoning, such a man will find himself glorying in the Lord (cf. 2 Cor. 10. 12–18).

v. 5   For each man will have to bear his own load.

Thus Paul announces the principle of individual responsibility: each man must carry his own pack (cf. v. 2). It is the business of every man to shoulder his own burden — to put his back under his own pack. Each man is called upon to take up his own particular sack which holds for him its own manageable weight. The apostle seems to be drawing into an intentional paradox this necessity with the requirement of verse 2. It is the man who admits the fact that he has his own burden to carry, who will be the most ready to help others to bear theirs.

(iii) Christian freedom induces liberality

Paul turns now to the question of the support of church teachers. Verse 6 links up with what has gone before, but at the same time opens up a new division of the subject, Thus would the apostle, as it were, arrest a former topic before it passes out of sight. The connection can be stated like this: though I insist on each man bearing his own burden, this must not be taken to mean that you are exempt from bearing the burden of caring for others, or from that of supporting those who serve you in the gospel. There is, then, a graduation of duties observable in the passage. There are responsibilities,

(a) to those who are down below us — the one overtaken in a fault; (b) to those who are round about us — one another; and (c) to those who are above us — him who teaches.

v. 6   Let him who is taught in the word share all good things with him who teaches.

The one who is taught is the 'catechumen', the person being instructed. As this instruction was orally given it was, perhaps, not limited to preaching in the assemblies, but probably extended to households and to individuals. From the very earliest times the sacred business of teaching believers was the divinely-commissioned task of selected men (cf. 1 Cor. 12. 28; Eph. 4. 11; 1 Thess. 5. 12; 1 Tim. 5. 17). The one taught is to 'impart a share' of his good things to the one who teaches. The teacher is 'to be let have a share in, what the taught possesses'. The 'goods' of the believer are 'good things' (cf. Lk 16. 25). The resemblance of the language here to 1 Cor. 9. 11 makes clear that Paul is speaking of imparting temporal goods; and in 2 Cor. 9. 6 the metaphor of 'sowing' and 'reaping' refers specifically to almsgiving.

v. 7   Do not be deceived; God is not mocked,

This, and the following verse, provide the general principle to which verse 6 is referred. There must be no mistake made about it (NEB), for none need be under any illusion (Phillips) that God can be 'taken in' by any empty profession. There is no hoodwinking of God: there can be no cock-a-snoot attitude when it comes to spiritual matters. To mock, is literally, 'to turn up the nose': and to try that on with God will not work.

for whatever a man sows, that he will also reap.

These words provide the norm to which life's actions are to be referred. They summarize both the law of the harvest and the the law of the hereafter. To sow life's 'good things' to the flesh, in selfish regard for oneself, instead of seeking to provide food for the soul and being willing to support those who provide it, is to try to pull the wool over God's eyes. But God is not blinded: it is such a man that is blinkered. For the natural law runs its appointed course in the spiritual world; so that what a man sows that he reaps. This is an ordained relationship, which God will not disturb or grace destroy.

v. 8 For he who sows to his own flesh will from the flesh reap corruption; but he who sows to the Spirit will from the Spirit reap eternal life.

The proverbial words of verse 7 are given a specific application in verse 8; verse 7 presents the kind of seed sown, this one, the nature of the soil into which the seed is cast. He who sows 'into' his flesh will have a harvest of like kind. Good seed sown in good soil assure a good harvest. The 'For' at the beginning of the verse has the force of 'because' — thus is the declaration a conclusion to be drawn. It is a statement which follows directly from the very nature of God and the operation of His laws.

There is a contrast between the 'his own flesh' and 'the Spirit'. The first locates the sowing in unrenewed human nature; the second sows in the Spirit and has thus the opportunity of producing the Spirit's 'fruit' (cf. 5. 22). When the Spirit is the soil and the sowing is done there, then the harvest reaped is eternal life. The phrase 'eternal life' is far less frequent in Paul than it is in the Johannine writings (cf. Rom. 2. 7; 5. 21; 6. 22, 23; 1 Tim. 1. 16; 6. 12; Tit. 1. 3; 3. 7). Eternal life is life of a spiritual quality, having the stamp of the divine approval, lived out here and now, and coming to full possession and reaching final perfection in the world to come. The reference to the

Spirit twice in the passage shows how both the spiritual harvesting here and the spiritual heaven hereafter, both depend upon Him. That reaping which authenticates a man's standing before God, and that standing before God from which the fruit of love, joy, peace and the like can blossom forth are of the Spirit.

v. 9 And let us not grow weary in well-doing,

Not only in the particular instance of verse 7 must beneficence continue; but there must be no tiring of doing good in general. Reaping and Sowing are not work in which one can relax. The exhortation is not to flag or faint. It is only in the untiring work of well-doing can one reach the undoubted verdict of doing-well. The words in the original present us with a verbal antithesis: 'in fair doing let us not show faint heart': 'in well doing let us not show ill heart'. The word for 'grow weary' (cf. Lk 18. 1; 2 Cor. 4. 1, 16; Eph. 3. 13; 2 Thess. 3. 13) has the idea of neglect by losing nerve. The counsel is then not to lose heart and thus to slacken hand.

for in due season we shall reap, if we do not lose heart.

At the proper season shall the reaping be done, and it shall be done to good purpose and result if we do not fatigue and fail. To relax effort (cf. Heb. 12. 3, 5), and to get oneself into a state of exhaustion (cf. Mt. 15. 32f.; Mk. 8. 3) would be fatal. In due time, is God's time; it is not the time of our due. For all is of grace; all is of the Spirit.

v, 10 So then, as we have opportunity, let us do good to all men,

By the use of the phrase 'So then' Paul would have us pause to take in what he has been saying, and then draw the inference. As we are to be workers of good for the sake of our fellow men our business is to be their benefactors. As, and when, the opportunity offers, we are 'to work for the good of all men' (NEB). Thus, in keeping with the whole spirit of his epistle, the apostle bids his readers to escape from a narrow particularism and a niggardly parochialism.

and especially to those who are of the household of faith.

These words are a sort of throw-back to the issue which has called forth the apostle's writing. The Galatians were on the verge of repudiating Paul as the apostle of faith, and those among them who stood with the apostle. The Judaizers had cut themselves off, and sought to cut off the Galatian believers from fellowship within the household of faith. Paul has shown how all who are justified are declared righteous by faith, are of the seed of Abraham and heirs of the promise. All such 'belong to the Christian household'; and are entitled to have the mutual care and concern of the Galatian Christians. But that can only be so if they acknowledge fully the way of faith. Concern for one another, and care for the needy, should characterize those who live and walk in the Spirit, for such are but the active demonstrations of faith. Such are the 'fruit' of the Spirit. Responsibility for other believers was evidently becoming more limited by the Galatians as the area of their fellowship was becoming more restricted. Paul had used his stirring and spiritual logic to remove the barriers which were being erected to fence off believer from believer; and by doing so he had advanced the area of opportunity for the working of good for members of the household of faith. 'Well-doing' is then the epitome of all that is involved in walking according to the faith-principle and working in the Spirit's power. And for those who sow to the Spirit, 'well-doing' will have its climax at the time of harvest in 'well-done'. So the believer, who may have sown in tears, will reap in joy.

A Concluding Section — Summary

In which Paul restates his Argument

6. 11-18

In these concluding verses, Paul again uncovers the motives of the Judaizers; they would escape persecution; they would boast in their position. But the apostle would make the cross of Christ his glory. He has not evaded the offence of the cross, for he has marks branded on his body to prove it. Before God, nothing counts, neither circumcision nor uncircumcision, but a new creation in Christ. This is the rule by which the true Israel of God walks: and upon such, peace and mercy shall rest.

11

THE CROSS AND THE COST

6. 11–18

(i) Heed the Letter I have written

v. 11   *See with what large letters I am writing to you with my own hand.*

This writing by the apostles in 'big letters' has led some to suggest that the conclusion only was penned by Paul. His reference to the large letters is then taken to be a humorous allusion to them, in contrast with the smaller writing of his amanuensis. The statement has then been used to support the speculation that he suffered from bad eyesight; the big letters being supposed to be a consequence of this handicap. There is certainly something to be said for the view that the apostle was in the habit of adding a closing paragraph, especially his benediction, in his own handwriting (cf. 2 Thess. 3. 17; 1 Cor. 16. 21; Col. 4. 18).

Whether, however, at this point in the Galatian letter the apostle took up his pen is less sure. Many commentators are convinced that so important was the subject and so instantaneous the character of the Galatian epistle that it must, from first to last, have come directly from the heart and by the hand of the apostle himself. In this case, the large letters may be taken as giving added emphasis to the concluding section. It appears to have been a centuries-old Eastern custom to lean heavily upon the pen when some emphatic declaration was to be specially noted. And so important does this closing section appear to be, that it could well justify the apostle using the method by which his parting message would be underscored for the special attention of his readers. The very boldness of the letters would serve to stress the firmness of the apostle's conviction and the force of his conclusion.

(ii) Heed the Message I have penned

v. 12 It is those who want to make a good showing in the flesh that would compel you to be circumcised,

By making circumcision morally obligatory upon Gentiles, the Judaizers were but unmasking their own perversity. Their aim was to put themselves in good standing with the religious world of Judaism. By their 'grand display in the flesh' (Moffatt), they exhibited a pretentious and grandiose adherence to outward religious ordinances. They conformed to the physical requirements of the Jewish law; but for the sake of appearances. By their showing 'in the flesh' they were exalting the flesh above the Spirit. They were indeed sowing to the flesh; and their reaping was predicted. They did not see that the flesh was to be crucified not circumcised.

and only in order that they may not be persecuted for the cross of Christ.

So there was their motive; their concern was not after all a high regard for the law, but a low regard for their own lives. They were not ready for the offence of the cross. They would escape persecution (cf. 5. 11). They would have Jesus as a Jewish Messiah; but with the Jewish element more prominent than the messianic. They proclaimed a ritual without a cross, so that they might possess a religion without a cost. But the cross is the very hub and heart of Paul's gospel (cf. 3. 1); and it was for this very reason that the Judaizers sought to undermine his apostleship and water down his message.

v. 13 For even those who receive circumcision do not themselves keep the law,

The Judaizers had convinced themselves of their zealous

keeping of the law. Paul explodes any protest from them that it is otherwise, with the firm declaration that they do not keep the law for all their profession of regard for it. For, if they did keep the law as the law should be kept, then they would have no need of the gospel. But there they are; wanting Christ in some measure and thereby showing that they have not fulfilled the laws demands in any measure. The apostle, however, is not raising again the question of whether it is possible for any to keep the law. He is pointing out, rather, that these teachers of circumcision, who seek to impose the rite, on the score that the law must be obeyed, do not themselves fulfil its demands. The inference is that they are not sincere in their teaching, because they only insist on that element which is conducive to their own advantage. In this one sentence the whole 'circumcision party' comes under condemnation.

but they desire to have you circumcised that they may glory in your flesh.

Instead of themselves keeping the law, they desire circumcision as an occasion for gaining credit with the Jews. By securing it they could exhibit their converts as wearing the badge of keepers of law. So would they be respected for their zeal for the traditions of the fathers. Thus would they escape persecution and gain plaudits. They desire to get the Galatians circumcised that they might glory in their flesh, and 'boast of your having submitted to that outward rite' (NEB).

v. 14   But far be it from me to glory except in the cross of our Lord Jesus Christ,

God forbid! (cf. 2. 17; 3. 21) exclaims the apostle; and the expression makes a contrast between God's way and man's. The Judaizers may 'glory' or 'boast' in the flesh; for Paul it will be 'in the cross'. Those of the circumcision might feast their eyes on the mutilated flesh of their deluded converts: Paul's gaze will be on the torn figure of Him who in His own body bore his sins to the tree. Paul set before his own eyes Christ as one crucified; and that One no less than the Lord Jesus Christ. Such a One was nailed there by the hands of sinners, but held there by a love divine — for love of him (cf. 2. 20). That was Paul's object of boast. That is most certainly what the Galatians knew; and in stating it again Paul would arouse his readers to a fresh appreciation of the cross, and recall to them how they had accepted what was done there by Christ, in the deed of the cross, as the all-sufficient basis of their salvation.

The 'our' before 'Lord Jesus Christ' serves to make the Galatians remember their oneness in fellowship with the apostle in the gospel, and the fact that they, no less than he, had reason for glorying in that same cross. Paul's boast is not in his own sufferings for Christ, but in Christ's sufferings for him.

by which the world has been crucified to me, and I to the world.

Paul sees the cross of the dying Lord Jesus Christ as holding for him a double crucifixion, that of the world to himself and of himself to the world. By the 'world', the apostle means the natural system of things which form the pattern, as it is itself formed by the presence, of unregenerate human nature (cf. 1 Cor. 2. 12; Eph. 2. 2; Js. 1. 27 etc.). Paul sees as nailed like a felon to the cross the world with its temporal interests, its sordid gains, its corruptible treasure, its passing show, its make-believe realities, and there dying by a certain and shameful, if lingering, death. There was Paul's old self left dying in Christ's death beyond the hope of recovery. Thus, for the apostle, is the world as good as dead to him and he to the world. There is no relationship of life between them any longer. Paul has indeed witnessed his own funeral; and leaving himself as dead at the cross, he has come to life in Christ.

'Paul speaketh here', comments Luther, 'of a high matter, and of great importance; that is, that every faithful man judgeth that to be wisdom, righteousness, and the power of God, which the world condemneth as the greatest folly, wickedness and weakness. And contrariwise, that which the world judgeth to be the highest religion, the service of God, the faithful know to be nothing else but execrable and horrid blasphemy against God. So the godly condemn the world, and the world condemneth the godly. But the godly have the right judgement on their side; for the spiritual man judgeth all things (1 Cor. 2. 15).'

v. 15   For neither circumcision counts for anything, nor uncircumcision, but a new creation.

In the world a Jew may boast of being a Jew and a Greek of being a Greek, but in Christ nothing matters, for whether one enters as a Jew or a Greek there is a 'new creation' (cf. 2 Cor. 5. 17). By thus eliminating every other reason for boasting, boasting in the cross alone stands out the more luminously. The pregnant phrase 'but a new creation' shows the transforming power of the cross. Circumcision is no help towards this result, and the absence of it is no hinderance. Both states are neutral, as far as justification is concerned. The particle 'for' points back to the argument running through the passage from verses 12 to 14. And it also seems to indicate a certain decisiveness in what the apostle has to say in this particular verse. His concern is to make clear that the one thing needful for all who would belong to the household of faith is the experience of a new creation. New life through the Spirit is the one thing that counts; this is the true circumcision of the heart (cf. Rom. 2. 29).

v. 16   Peace and mercy be upon all who walk by this rule,

Upon all who guide their steps and march together (same word as in 5. 25) by this rule shall peace and mercy abide. Those under this 'rule' are the 'new creation' in Christ, in contrast with those who attach significance to externals. The word for rule referred originally to a carpenter's rod, and here is used metaphorically to mean a model or pattern (cf. 2 Cor. 10. 13, 16). The rule or principle for true believers is either the experience of becoming a new creation (v. 15), or the realization of the significance of the cross (v. 14). But perhaps both concur in the apostle's thought. For it is in the realization of the cross as the place of death, that the reality of the new creation comes about. It is from Golgotha, the place of crucifixion, that there blossoms red life that shall endless be.

upon the Israel of God.

These words echo the benediction, 'peace upon Israel', with which the Septuagint version of Psalms 115 and 128 close.

Israel was the sacred name for the Jews as a nation under the theocracy. By adding the limiting qualification 'of God', the apostle would distinguish between 'Israel after the flesh' and the spiritual Israel. All along, Paul has been arguing that those united with Christ by faith are Abraham's true sons, and heirs of the promise. This one designation summarizes all that he has said; and includes the whole company of believers, whether Jews or Gentiles.

v. 17   Henceforth let no man trouble me;

Paul pleads that no man should 'cause trouble' to him further. He is not asking to be exempted from burdens, for he has stated that it is required of all believers that they bear their own burdens and share those of others. What the apostle wants to be free of is that heavy anxiety which pressed upon him because of the Judaizers' perversion of the gospel. Of that he would rid; it was a burden which should never have been added to his already anxious concern for all the churches (cf. 2 Cor. 11. 28). Paul has now no more to say. He has spoken his first word as an authoritative apostle, and now his last as a tested servant.

for I bear on my body the marks of Jesus.

What were the marks, the brands which the apostle had scarred on his body? Some would interpret the word in a figurative and some in a literal sense. Thus, there are those who see in the statement a reference to the custom of slaves being branded by their master as a sign of ownership, or the brands by which they were set aside for temple service. Inscriptions in Galatia about 'sacred slaves' is thought to lend support to this letter idea. In rare cases, captives were branded by their captors, and often soldiers tattooed on their arm the name of their favourite general. It would seem, however, that the reference is to actual bodily marks received by the apostle in the service of Christ. They were visible marks of persecution nobly borne. 2 Cor. 11. 23–27 gives a catalogue of the things Paul had to endure for Christ's sake (cf. 1 Cor. 15. 32). Acts 16. 19f. records how Paul was stoned at Lystra, and left for dead (cf. 13. 45, 50). Cogent would be Paul's reference to those very marks which he had received in their midst, and which they would, doubtless, have seen with their own eyes. His allusion to them would be an argument for his desire for them in the past, and hope for them in the present. Would not such scars be eloquent of his regard for them? Could he not let them speak for him? Yet the scars were not uncovered by Paul to parade his standing, but to persuade them from slipping. Made visible and vocal in them, had they but the eyes to see and the ears to hear, was the actuality of the cross. In the wounds of Jesus, his own wounds were taken up and transformed.

The Grace Blessing

v. 18   The grace of our Lord Jesus Christ be with your spirit, brethren, Amen

So the epistle, which had begun abruptly with expostulation by Paul, the apostle, ends effectionately from Paul, the brother. Such is characteristic of him. The word grace is significant at the end of his letter, as it is at the beginning (cf. 1. 3); for from first to last, Paul's theme was grace. In neither place has the term a mere conventional use, for at every mention of this word the apostle is summarizing the essential message of the gospel given to him by the revelation of God. Grace will, therfore, be among his last words, as his celestial symphony dies away.

And it is the grace of our Lord Jesus Christ — His grace, for there is no grace found elsewhere — grace, as God's very 'radiant adequacy' for man's helpless deficiency. He is 'ours' says Paul, so giving the Galatians a parting reminder of their common unity and their united community in Christ. Such grace is to be with their spirit. Paul puts it this way, perhaps, because of the carnal nature of Judaizing religion (cf. Philem. 25; 2 Tim. 4. 22). With an affectionate 'brethren' and a reverential 'Amen' the epistle of freedom in faith closes. For Paul never allowed his burdens to hinder his blessing; nor his duties to destroy his devotion.